SCOTLAND

In 1895, Slains Castle, at that time the seat of the 19th Earl of Errol, was Bram Stoker's inspiration for the horror novel "Dracula". The castle, now in ruins, overlooks the North Sea near Aberdeen.

FASCINATING EARTH
SCOTLAND

The distinctive colours and patterns of a tartan kilt usually identify the wearer's association with a particular clan. Both the formal tartan kilt and a casual kilt in other fabrics may be worn.

ABOUT THIS BOOK

Scottish pride in the country and its many traditions, including a history of bold technological innovation, is legendary – and it is also charming, because it does not leave visitors out in the cold but rather embraces them as welcome guests. Scots' hospitality is often demonstrated in a spontaneous invitation to visitors to tour the incredibly beautiful countryside or enjoy a beer or whisky with their hosts in a pub.

A trip through Scotland's history must begin with an excursion into prehistory – the earliest evidence of hunter-gatherers so far north dates back to 7000 BC. Thousands of years later, Scottish clan chiefs battled for supremacy of the broad, rugged country. In the Highlands alone, there were some 180 clans, who were engaged in constant feuding. They held the arable land farmed by crofters, made pacts with the royal families of Europe while engaging in intrigues against them, and built fortresses and castles to demonstrate their power. Thus, the buildings that today are so steeped in history and typical of Scotland were erected in the midst of grand scenery – history and landscape are superlatively united in this country.

This northernmost part of Britain is currently home to a population of roughly five million – the Scots' strong ties to their beloved country with its mountains, lochs and rugged coasts have never been broken. Tradition and progress go hand in hand in Scotland: efficient oil extraction, state-of-the-art ship-building, high tech from "Silicon Glen", Dolly the cloned sheep – Scotland is a fascinating blend of nature and technology, history and trendiness, which always, however, retains its unique character.

This guide presents the riches that are Scotland. The atlas section that follows makes it easy to find the places and sights you want to see and adds a wealth of pointers useful for visitors. The index at the end, linking the picture section and the atlas pages, also includes the Internet addresses of the most important sights so you can get your bearings more quickly. Discover the magic of Scotland in all its diversity.

The Publisher

Sheep are everywhere in Scotland: be they Scottish Blackface Sheep in the Highlands or the prehistoric "Soay Sheep" on St Kilda. The sheep auction in Lairg is the largest of its kind in Europe.

CONTENTS

The wild grandeur of Scotland extends from its wave-lashed northerly tip to the hill country of the Southern Uplands and the Border Country in the south between Scotland and England. If you don't mind defying all sorts of weather and know how to dress for it, you'll warm the cockles of your hosts' hearts. The best months for visiting are May, June and September – and August is a must for all Festival fans.

A highlight of the Heart of Neolithic Orkney World Heritage Site
is the Ring o' Brodgar (below left),
a stone circle dating back some
5,000 years. Of the original 60
monoliths, fewer than 30 remain
standing. The Shetland archipelago
consists of about 100 islands.
Every walk here is rewarded with
stunning views, such as that from
the cliffs of Herma Ness at the
northern tip of Unst (below right).

THE ORKNEY AND SHETLAND ISLANDS, THE HEBRIDES

Off the north-west coast of Scotland lie the Inner and Outer Hebrides, a group of more than 500 islands. Volcanic rock, slate and gneiss, grasslands, moors and over 100 lochs are the principal features of this rugged, primal landscape, where the northern climate is tempered by the Atlantic gulf stream. Only one-fifth of the islands are inhabited, by a total of around 60,000 people who make their living from tourism, fishing and raising sheep and cattle. Further round the coast, the sea is dotted with the dramatic Orkneys and Shetland Islands.

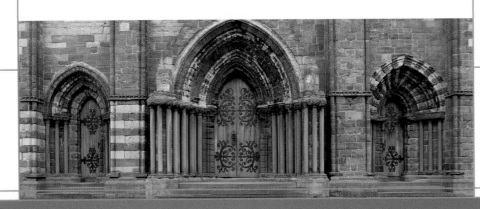

The harbour of Kirkwall (Old Norse "kirkjuvagr" = "Church Bay") (below), the capital of the Orkneys' main island. St Magnus, Kirkwall (right and below right) is the only Scottish cathedral to have survived the Reformation intact. A music festival is held here each June.

Mainland (Orkney Islands)

At its narrowest point, Mainland – the largest of some 70 islands in the Orkney archipelago – is only 2.5 km (1.5 miles) wide. On this neck of land lies Kirkwall, the island's principal town and home to many of the 20,000 or so "Orcadians". There are ferry links to mainland Scotland and to most of the other Orkney islands from this austerely beautiful harbour. One of the finest island towns in Scotland, Kirkwall has a rich collection of 16th- and 17th-century buildings. Dominating the skyline is St Magnus Cathedral, founded in 1137 by Earl Rognvald in memory of his uncle, Magnus Erlendsson, Earl of Orkney, who was murdered and later canonised. Both Magnus and Rognvald are buried here. The massive Norman columns supporting the 75-m (246-ft) long nave of the cathedral, which was not completed until the late 15th century, are an impressive sight.

Typical of northern and western coastal Scotland and the islands are the circular dry-stone towers called "brochs" – Iron Age constructions used either as forts or as fortified homesteads. The Broch of Gurness (right) and the Neolithic settlement of Skara Brae (below) are both on the Orkney Mainland.

GRAND TESTIMONY TO A VANISHED CULTURE

Mainland, the main island in the Orkneys, is home to Britain's largest collection of prehistoric monuments – you can visit the many megalithic sites only on foot or by bicycle. Remains of Viking settlements also survive on this place. The greatest attraction, however, is Skara Brae, Europe's best-preserved Neolithic settlement, about 16 km (10 miles) north of Stromness. The area of Skara Brae was probably settled continuously from 3200 to 2200 BC, when its Neolithic inhabitants may have been the victims of a natural disaster, such as a sudden climate change. This prehistoric settlement then remained hidden beneath sand dunes for 4,000 years until, in 1850, it was exposed during a severe storm. Excavations carried out later revealed an almost complete village. The numerous artifacts found here make it possible to reconstruct the lives led by Neo-lithic peoples in northern Europe. The inhabitants of Skara Brae made stone furniture, presumably because there was no wood even then on this virtually treeless island, although it could be that this was a place of cult observance. The Neolithic village would have sustained about 30 people, living as self-sufficient farmers and herdsmen – there are no indications of trading with nearby communities. In 1999, many of the Neolithic ruins were designated a UNESCO World Heritage Site.

A low entrance passage lined with huge stone slabs leads to the main chamber of Maes Howe (below). The runes on the walls of this chambered cairn and passage grave are called "Viking graffiti" (right). The cairn is 35 m (115 ft) in diameter and is well protected by a thick mantle of turf (inset).

IN THE NEOLITHIC REALM OF THE DEAD

Viking invaders settled the Orkneys from the 8th century, leaving behind many traces of their presence that are still visible today. A good example is the runes carved on the stones of Maes Howe, a prehistoric chambered cairn and passage grave, today the best preserved of its kind in western Europe. Dating to 2700 BC, Maes Howe is located about 10 km (6 miles) west of Kirkwall on the Mainland. This 7-m (23-ft) high grassy cairn, or artificial mound, rising out of a field, is evidence of how Neolithic people buried the dead. The tomb is entered through an 11-m (36-ft) tunnel leading into a main chamber and three side chambers. The runic graffiti on the walls suggest that the Vikings looted treasure when they raided the cairn in the 12th century. The main chamber is rectangular, with a buttressed corbel-vaulted roof; the technical mastery of its architect is demonstrated in the drystone construction with its fine jointwork. The evening of the winter solstice reveals a special feature of this tomb and cult place – the entrance is precisely aligned with the point at which the sun sets on this symbolic day, so that the sun's rays illuminate the rear wall of the chamber. Excavations in the 19th century were hampered by a large slab that separated the main chamber from the tunnel.

Rackwick Bay, Hoy (below). This quiet island offers scope for individualists such as farmer Terry Thomson (right), whose vintage car is ideal for touring the island. The north coast has stunning cliffs (inset right), as well as the sandstone sea stack known as the "Old Man of Hoy" (inset left).

Hoy

The second largest of the Orkneys is Hoy, a name derived from the Old Norse word "Haey", meaning "high island" – at 479 m (1,571 ft), Hoy's Ward Hill is the highest point in the island group. Hoy also has some of Britain's most northerly natural woodlands. The island is divided into two very different regions, connected by a causeway – the gently rolling south, used for agriculture, and the hilly north with its breathtaking cliffs.

A spectacular Orkney landmark is St John's Head, at 364 m (1,135 ft) one of the highest cliffs in Britain. Visitors to the island – most of them birdwatchers and lovers of unspoilt nature – take the three-hour walk from the village of Rackwick to the imposing cliffs. From here, you look down on the "Old Man of Hoy", a red sandstone stack rising from the sea to a height of 137 m (450 ft), which is a popular challenge for climbers.

The Standing Stones of Stenness (below and inset right) and the Ring o' Brodgar (inset left) are celebrated prehistoric monuments. The small tidal island of Brough Birsay (right), once the seat of Orkney's political and religious power, is only accessible by causeway at low tide from Mainland's north-west coast.

TIME-TRAVEL IN MAGICAL REALMS

The four tall Stone Age monoliths standing near the village of Stenness on the Orkney Mainland are almost 5,000 years old. In the Neolithic period, they formed a circle of twelve standing stones with a diameter of 30 m (98 ft). The stones remaining today are irregularly distributed; the tallest is more than 5 m (16 ft) high. Not far from the Standing Stones of Stenness is the "Ring o' Brodgar", an even larger stone circle and henge monument built on a westward-sloping plateau on the Ness o' Brodgar. The most celebrated Neolithic monument on the Orkneys, the Ring o' Brodgar was originally composed of 60 monoliths in a circle with a diameter of almost 104 m (341 ft), each stone standing between 2 m and 4.5 m (7 ft and 15 ft) high. Today, only 27 stones remain standing. One of them bears a runic inscription from the Viking era, spelling the Nordic name "Bjørn". It is not clear whether these prehistoric stone circles were once used as places of assembly, or were erected for ritual sacrifice or worship, or even as lunar observatories that helped the Neolithic peoples to create a precise calendar. What is certain, however, is the mystery and enchantment of these great monoliths silhouetted in the evening light against a backdrop of cloud and sea – a sight that never fails to captivate visitors.

The cliffs round Esha Ness lighthouse in the north of the Shetland mainland (below). The Shetland Woollen Company (right) has a workshop and showroom in the old island capital of Scalloway. You can shop here for knitwear and watch the intricate patterns emerge on Shetland sweaters.

Mainland (Shetland Islands)

Lying off the north-east coast of Scotland, the Shetlands consist of more than 100 islands, of which only 15 are inhabited. The rocky coasts of this narrow archipelago, which is about 100 km (62 miles) long, are even more spectacular than those of Orkney. The largest of the Shetland Islands, like the biggest of the Orkneys, is known as Mainland. The Shetlands' administrative centre and the only town on Mainland is Lerwick, with an airport, ferry connections and a population of around 7,500. The elongated southern tip of the island consists of moors and arable land; most of the archaeological sites are also here. The central region is dotted with woodland, while the west and north are rugged with moors and jagged coastal cliffs. Along with sheep-farming, fishing and aquaculture, the economy of the Shetland Islands is boosted by the offshore oil industry.

Although small in height, the famous Shetland ponies are among the sturdiest of all equines. Look out for them in the wild on the Shetland Mainland (below), as well as on Unst and Yell. Shetland sheep have short, springy fleeces and represent a vital source of income for many Shetland farmers (right).

SHETLAND SHEEP AND SHETLAND PONIES

Shetland sheep are thought to descend from ovines brought to the islands by the Vikings. Their hard-wearing, springy wool is woven into rustic tweed yarn, while the one-ply "cobweb" or delicate two-ply yarn is also used for making the distinctive knitted Shetland lace. The primal ancestors of the diminutive Shetland ponies are said to have been Tundra horses, which were widespread in Scandinavia more than 10,000 years ago and migrated from there to the Shetlands before the end of the last ice age. Their numbers are now, unfortunately, diminishing on Shetland – only about 2,000 remain. Pony bones have been found dating back to the 2nd century AD. Despite their small size (only 70–100 cm/28–39 in tall), these ponies are very strong and for a long time were used in agriculture and as pit ponies in mining. Today, the hardy, long-lived Shetlands are popular as children's riding ponies and for carriage driving. Half-wild ponies only live in the north of the Shetland island of Mainland, as well as on Unst and Yell, two other Shetland islands. To see Shetland ponies in their natural setting, go to a "ferist" – a Scandinavian term for a cattle grid in the road – and wait where you see a "Careful – ponies" sign – these wild animals are curious and might be persuaded to overcome their shyness…

Unst is a wildlife sanctuary with only about 1,000 human inhabitants. At the northern tip, the Atlantic pounds the gneiss cliffs of the Hermaness National Nature Reserve, home to numerous puffins (below). In the sea around the island live seals, porpoises and otters (right).

Unst

About one degree latitude north of the Orkneys, the Shetland Islands, with Unst at the northern tip of the archipelago, are as far north as you can go in Britain. Unst's scenic diversity includes cliffs, sheltered coves and sandy beaches, tussocks of heather and expanses of grey stone. The Hermaness National Nature Reserve is home to seabirds in their hundreds of thousands – puffins, the world's second-largest colony of the rare great skua, and even a solitary black-browed albatross, named Albert. Botanists also find plenty to discover on the island, which is the habitat of some 400 species of flora. Other highlights of Unst are 16th-century Muness Castle and the old harbour with its traditional fishing boats and an exhibition on seafaring – if you are lucky, you might persuade an old fisherman, now a museum custodian, to "spin you a yarn".

A visitor footpath leads to the prehistoric site on the south coast of the Shetland Mainland known as Jarlshof (right), where you can time-travel through 4,000 years of settlement history. The complex includes a village of round houses as well as two "souterrains", used for cold storage (below).

JARLSHOF – FROM THE ICE AGE TO THE 17TH CENTURY

The most significant archaeological site in the Shetland Islands is Jarlshof at the southern tip of Mainland. This prehistoric settlement complex includes typical Bronze Age and Iron Age round houses but also incorporates Viking longhouses. The earliest part of the settlement, with some small oval houses, is located on the eastern fringe of the broad complex. Stone tools found here indicate that the prehistoric inhabitants caught and processed seals and whales. The complex also includes a Bronze Age smithy, an Iron Age broch (a dry-stone defensive tower or fort), a village of round houses from the same period, and two small "souterrains" – underground chambers used primarily as cold-storage facilities for settlement provisions. The most recent buildings are a medieval farmstead and the 17th-century seat of the earls Robert and Patrick Stewart. Thus Jarlshof spans more than 4,000 years of settlement history, between 2500 BC and about 1600 AD. It was Sir Walter Scott, the celebrated Scottish author of historic novels, who gave this extraordinary settlement its name. On a visit to the Stewart manor in 1816, he saw the ruins, which had recently been uncovered by violent storms, and later immortalised them in his famous novel "The Pirate" under the name that they still bear.

The harbour of Stornaway, the only town on Lewis (below). Lewis and Harris together form "Long Island" (opposite). Right: peat cutters on Lewis and North Uist.
Below, from left: near Horgabost (Harris); Butt of Lewis; crofters' houses on Harris and at Garynahine (Lewis). Below, inset: St Clement's Church, Harris.

The Hebrides

There are more than 500 islands in the Hebrides, the archipelago that protects north-western Scotland from the Atlantic. Their coastlines are fissured from the constant assault of surf and there are many sandy beaches in sheltered coves. About 80 of the islands are inhabited. The Inner Hebrides lie closer to the mainland; the largest and most important are Skye, Mull, Iona, Islay, Jura, Rum, Eigg, Coll, Tiree and Colonsay. Further out in the Atlantic, the Outer Hebrides, known as the Western Isles, form a 210-km (130-mile) arc. The main islands are Lewis and Harris, North Uist, Benbecula, South Uist and Barra. Lewis and Harris (known as "Long Island") are linked by a narrow strip of land. The administrative centre for the Western Isles is Stornoway, the only town on Lewis; the Inner Hebrides form part of the Highland region that includes Argyll and Bute.

The legendary stone circle of Callanish (below and right) is an enchantingly enigmatic landmark on the Western Isles. It is said that some of the stones – which are of Lewisian gneiss, striated with veins of white or black quartz – radiate energy. Visitors enjoy trying this out for themselves…

STANDING STONES OF CALLANISH

The monoliths of Callanish, standing west of Stornoway on the island of Lewis, are probably Scotland's most beautiful stone circle – yet for many hundreds of years, this prehistoric site was almost entirely buried in peat. Today, a total of 47 menhirs still stand. Dating from between 3,000 and 1,500 BC, the monoliths, made of native Lewis gneiss, were set up in phases. The circle is approached by a long avenue of standing stones to the north, with shorter, single rows – possibly incomplete avenues – to the south, west and east, forming the shape of a Celtic cross or "sun cross". The 82-m (90-yd) long north avenue is stunning – two parallel rows of standing stones, about 8 m (9 yds) apart. At the centre of the circle (11–13 m/ 12–14 yd wide) of 13 standing stones is one huge central stone, which is 5 m (16 ft) high and weighs about 5 tonnes (5.5 tons). This monolith marks the western boundary of a small burial cairn, believed to have been added at a later date, where the remains from several inhumations were found. The megalithic cult site at Callanish stands comparison with Stonehenge in the south of England and is regarded as the landmark of the Western Isles. It has been suggested that the entire complex may have been an astronomical observatory or the basis of a lunar calendar system.

The coastline of Berneray (below). On South Uist, a cairn marks the birthplace of Flora MacDonald, who in 1746 aided the escape of Bonnie Prince Charlie, the Stuart pretender to the English throne (right). View of North Uist from Eaval (far right). The island of Barra (inset left); Castlebay, Barra's main village (inset right).

Berneray, North Uist, South Uist and Barra

Empty beaches, coves and rugged rock, restful and peaceful on still days, violent and elemental in stormy weather – the Outer Hebrides are a fascinating world apart, even for Scots. The lovely little island of Berneray lies between Harris and North Uist in the Sound of Harris. The principal town on North Uist is Lochmaddy; the west coast has dramatic cliffs, magnificent sandy beaches and the fertile raised beaches known as "machair", a Hebridean phenomenon created by a drop in sea level, leaving in this case a carpet of meadow flowers. In summer, ferries run between Oban and South Uist, the second largest island in the Outer Hebrides, whose main town is Lochboisdale. Barra, the main island of the most southerly group in the Outer Hebrides, includes Vatersay, which, like Barra, is inhabited, and smaller uninhabited islands.

The traditional early 20th-century wooden looms are still humming in the island cottage-industry workshops as weavers on the islands of Lewis and Harris, Uist and Barra use wool from island sheep to make fine Harris Tweed cloth in the classic muted tones for which it is famous.

TWEED: HARD-WEARING AUTHENCITY

The words "Hand-woven Harris Tweed" written above the orb emblem of the Harris Tweed Authority certifies the authenticity of the Western Isles' most famous export. To be genuine, sturdy Harris Tweed must be made of Scottish wool, spun and dyed on the Outer Hebrides and hand-woven by islanders in the local cottage industry.

This time-consuming and work-intensive craft is still carried out on Lewis and Harris, Uist and Barra. For centuries, the islanders made this rugged cloth of pure wool for their own use, as a sort of "second skin" to protect them from the windy, damp and cold climate of their native region. However, when Lady Dunmoore discovered

"Clò Mór" (the Gaelic name for Harris Tweed), in the mid-19th century, the tweed industry was born on the Scottish mainland and then in England as well. Soon, factory-made Harris Tweed was available everywhere; but quality standards varied considerably. In 1993, the Harris Tweed Authority in Stornoway (Lewis) was

granted the sole rights to Harris tweed by the original Harris Tweed Association, which had been incorporated in 1909. Since then, consistent quality and the exclusive use of the trademark that guarantees the origin of this distinctively flecked luxury cloth in the Outer Hebrides have been strictly monitored.

Portree (Gaelic Porth Righ = King's port), Skye's administrative centre (below), was allegedly given this name after James V landed there in 1540; before this, it had been Kiltragleann (church of St Talarican in the glen). It has a population of around 2,000. Elgol (right) is a small village in southern Skye.

Isle of Skye

Now that a bridge connects Kyle of Lochalsh on the Scottish mainland to Skye, the largest of the Inner Hebrides is more popular than ever. With an area of almost 1,735 sq km (1,866 sq ft), Skye provides marvellous walking and climbing opportunities, notably in the spectacular Black Cuillin range in the south. The population of 8,000 lives mainly from tourism. The jagged coastline of Skye gave rise to the Gaelic name "Eilean Sgiathanach", the Winged Isle; it has also been called "Eilean a' Cheò" – Isle of Mist. Almost half of the islanders still speak Gaelic and there is a centre for Gaelic courses. It was the Vikings who called the island "Skùyo", Old Norse for "sky". At the Royal Hotel in Portree, Bonnie Prince Charlie, fleeing to France in 1746, said farewell to Flora MacDonald, who is still revered as an island heroine.

The curious landscape of the Quiraing massif (below right). Skye looks irresistible beneath a cloudless sky (right). The most remarkable buildings on the St Kilda archipelago, uninhabited since 1930, are "cleitean" – domed dry-stone huts, some of them prehistoric, once used as storage facilities (bottom left).

Isle of Skye and St Kilda

Skye is heaven for both walkers and experienced climbers. One spectacular place for rock climbing is the Quiraing massif – shaped by landslips from the Trotternish Ridge in the far north of the island, grotesque basalt formations with names like The Needle, The Table and The Prison are its distinctive feature. The St Kilda archipelago, also of volcanic origin and settled more than 2,000 years ago but uninhabited since 1930, is located about 66 km (41 miles) west of Benbecula (Outer Hebrides, between North and South Uist). Its four storm-lashed islands – Dun, Soay, Boreray and Hirta – escaped glaciation in the last ice age and so retained their unique scenery, which ensured them UNESCO World Natural Heritage status in 1986. Stunningly steep cliffs provide excellent nesting for rare birds, including the world's largest colonies of northern fulmar, northern gannet and puffins.

The spectacular basalt columns of the Isle of Staffa (below, centre right and far right) were formed by a layer of lava cooling more slowly than those above and below. The island is home to numerous seabirds, including hundreds of puffins (right). A visit to the inspiring Fingal's Cave is a must (inset).

Isle of Staffa

A geological marvel of black basalt, the Isle of Staffa can only be reached by boat from Mull or Iona – weather conditions permitting. As the legend goes, this island (only 200 x 600 m/219 x 656 yds) represents the "Scottish end" of the Giant's Causeway in Northern Ireland, which originally linked the two places but was destroyed, according to legend, by two battling giants. A visit to Fingal's Cave, named after a hero of Celtic myth, is an extraordinary experience – its interior reminiscent of a cathedral, the cave is 75 m (246 ft) long. Its Gaelic name, An Uaimh Binn – the melodious cave – refers to the musical echoes of the waves breaking in on its dark rock walls. Scandinavian dramatists and British poets, the painter J.M.W. Turner and the German composer Mendelssohn ("The Hebrides Overture") were inspired here by the unrivalled spectacle of the elements.

The gleaming white lighthouse is a prominent landmark on the Isle of Mull (below). Around 2,400 people live on the island, some 800 of them in Tobermory (right). Bunessan, at the southern tip of the island, has a traditional grocer's shop (centre right). A ferry service links the islands of Mull and Iona (far right).

Isle of Mull

The Isle of Mull, which has a coastline more than 480 km (298 miles) long, is noted for its rugged, hilly scenery and karst mountain ranges – the highest peak is Ben More, at 966 m (3,170 ft). There are three ferry routes for cars and passengers running between Mull and the Scottish mainland, but the most popular is still the line from Oban. Birdwatchers may be lucky enough to spot golden eagles, white-tailed eagles or merlin falcons on the island. Walks on Mull lead to attractive landmarks such as the white lighthouse. At Tobermory there is a small whisky distillery, which has been closed and reopened several times since it was founded in 1798 and was again revived in 1990 after a ten-year closure. The historic Isle of Mull Railway carries visitors 2 km (1.25 miles) from the Old Pier ferry terminal in Craignure to the early Victorian Torosay Castle.

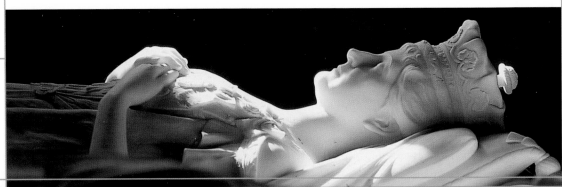

More than 60 Scottish, Norwegian and Irish kings have found their final resting place in the Benedictine abbey church on Iona (below and far right, below). A sarcophagus in the abbey (right); a tombstone in the cloister (inset); St Martin's Cross stands opposite the west portal of the abbey (far right, above).

Isle of Iona

The island of Iona lies off the southern tip of Mull. The exiled Irish missionary monk St Columba landed on this former Druidic island in 563 and founded a monastery here. From Iona he and his companions set out to convert Scotland to Christianity. Columba died in 597 and the island became a place of pilgrimage. Ravaged by a series of Viking incursions, which began in 794, the monastery was rebuilt several times. Around 1200, Reginald MacDonald founded Iona Abbey, a Benedictine establishment, on the site of the earlier abbey church. The 13th-century Norman chancel and parts of the chapel have survived. The abbey was restored in the 20th century by the Iona Cathedral Trust and the Iona Community. St Martin's Cross (4.3 m/14 ft high) dates from the 8th century and is almost perfectly preserved. It stands opposite the abbey's west portal.

The coastal holiday resort of Dornoch (below) is the ideal place for enjoying both the beach and some legendary golf courses, such as the Royal Dornoch Golf Club course dating from 1616.

If you want to learn about the traditional Scottish way of life, stay in a cottage in the Highlands – many Highlanders let rooms and offer self-catering holiday accommodation (inset).

IN THE HIGHLANDS

Most people think of the Highlands when they think of Scotland. Less exposed to English influence than those regions nearer the border, the thinly settled Highlands were divided up among the clans for centuries. The Highland culture, briefly proscribed following the union with England, has survived. With rugged mountains, quiet valleys and lochs lacing the west coast, the Highlands are a paradise for walkers, who can observe their flora and fauna undisturbed – after all, only about four per cent of Scotland's population lives here.

Sweeping Sandwood Bay (below) is popular with surfers. South of the Duncansby Head peninsula near Caithness, the Duncansby Stacks rise from the sea, sculpted by wind and waves to an unusual conical shape (right). Clò Mór Cliffs at Cape Wrath are Britain's highest cliffs at 281 m (922 ft) (inset).

Clo Mor Cliffs, Duncansby Stacks and Sandwood Bay

In 1828, Robert Stevenson, father of famed "Treasure Island" author Robert Louis Stevenson, built a lighthouse at Cape Wrath, whose name – appropriate though it is in English – means "Turning Point" in Old Norse because Viking ships would turn for home from here. At 281 m (922 ft) Britain's highest cliffs, the Clò Mór Cliffs drop sheer to the sea at the lighthouse. When visibility is good, from here you can see west as far as Harris and Lewis in the Hebrides and even the Orkneys to the east. The bizarre Duncansby Stacks rising from the sea at Duncansby Head have been sculpted by wind, weather and waves. This region has exceptionally good sandy beaches – the most northerly is Sandwood Bay near Kinlochbervie, one of Scotland's most important fishing harbours. Surfers rave about the South Seas atmosphere and conditions prevailing in this expansive bay.

Cul Mòr (850 m/2,789 ft) is a
challenge for climbers (below, top).
The road to Ullapool passes the
picturesque Loch Lurgainn (below).
There is a glorious view from the
peak of Ben More over Coigach,
Stac Pollaidh (Stack Polly), Cul Mòr
and Suilven (right).

Inverpolly Nature Reserve

Lonely lochs (the term almost always refers to saltwater fjords rather than freshwater lakes) and rugged rock distinguish the rather remote mountainous region of Inverpolly, about 30 km (19 miles) north of Ullapool. In the early 1960s, the region was declared a nature reserve and is certainly worth visiting. Here, a number of scenic trails – such as the 1.6-km (1-mile) Nature Trail that starts at the Visitor Center – take you through a diverse landscape of mountain, moor, wood and loch. Badgers, deer, the European otter and more than 100 bird species populate this nature reserve. The mountain flora of this beautiful region is also particularly diverse, while geologists are fascinated by Knockan Crag where a thrust fault, the first ever recognised, reversed the formation of the cliff strata so that older rocks lie over much younger ones.

The lovely landscape around Loch Assynt (below). Loch Assynt (right) is famous for salmon and trout fishing. About 100,000 tonnes (98,400 tons) of fish are landed annually in Ullapool harbour (far right). This view of Loch Broom (inset) resembles a Kokoschka painting.

Around Ullapool

This pretty little coastal town in the thinly settled Western Highlands is the largest settlement for miles around, even though it has only about 1,300 inhabitants. Established as a herring harbour on Loch Broom by the British Fisheries Association in 1788, Ullapool is still a major fishing harbour and ferry terminal, with ferries departing for Lewis in the Outer Hebrides. In 1940, Ullapool was a refuge for the Austrian Expressionist painter Oskar Kokoschka. Paintings featuring the beautiful broad expanse of scenic Loch Broom recall his stay here. The tourist infrastructure in Ullapool is excellent – a small museum in a deconsecrated church explains local history and there are several hotels, a swimming pool, many pubs, gift shops and even an annual music festival. Boat trips to seal colonies and salmon farms are particularly popular with visitors.

Eilean Donan Castle, a medieval fortress (below and right), is situated on Loch Duich in Glen Shiel (below, top). This magnificent setting has been used as a location for major box-office hits such as "Highlander", "Loch Ness", "Braveheart" and the 19th James Bond film, "The World is Not Enough".

Eilean Donan Castle

The legendary Eilean Donan Castle stands at the confluence of three saltwater lochs and is probably Scotland's most photographed architectural motif. The castle is located in Glen Shiel, with the mountains on Loch Duich as a spectacular backdrop, and is reached by either a causeway or a stone footbridge. Alexander II of Scotland built the first fortress on the site in 1220 as a defence against the Vikings. Later, it came into the possession of Clan MacKenzie (later the Earls of Seaforth), who left their protectors and constables, the MacReas, in charge. Destroyed in 1719 by three English frigates because Spanish troops were garrisoned there, Eilean Donan was carefully restored between 1919 and 1932 by a member of Clan MacRea. The castle museum is a good source of information on the turbulent history of this commanding fortress.

Red-haired "monsters" with endearing faces – the shaggy, long-horned Highland cattle are famed far beyond the borders of Scotland for their good nature and their rugged good looks. Gourmets worldwide appreciate this gentle native Highland breed for the succulent, lean beef it yields.

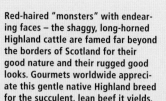

KYLOE: SCOTTISH HIGHLAND CATTLE

Stoic, sturdy and self-reliant – Kyloe (Lowland Scots) or Highland cattle have been bred in the Highlands and western Scotland for at least two centuries in their present long-horned form. The registry – a "herd book" containing all the essential breeders' data for identifying these animals – has existed since 1884, but the breed is one of the most ancient in the world. The earliest mention of Highland cattle in Scotland dates from the 6th century. Whether the "Heelan Coo" is really native to Scotland or was imported from Scandinavia by the Vikings is still a matter of dispute among experts. Either way, it is well adapted indeed to the harsh living conditions prevailing in Britain's far north. Drenched by heavy rainfall and lashed by severe storms, Highland cattle spend their summers on stony ground feeding on thistles and survive long, harsh winters without extra fodder and warm byres. The thick, shaggy reddish-brown pelt enables Highland cattle to endure cold up to -30° C (-22° F), so they are fully free-range all year round in the Highlands. Raising cattle and sheep (for meat and wool) is one of the four pillars of Scottish agriculture, alongside dairy farming, intensive agriculture, and traditional crofter small-holdings producing crops such as barley, oats, rapeseed and potatoes.

Exotic plants from around the world thrive in Inverewe Garden (below). Left: Inverewe Garden (top); sub-tropical New Zealand oleander (second and third pictures); rhodo-dendron (fourth and fifth pictures). Loch Maree (right) stretches far inland.

Loch Maree and Inverewe Garden

Loch Maree, a long, deep trough lake formed by ice age glaciers, is a highlight of the north-west coast. Otters and black-throated divers (Arctic loons) fish in the nutrient-rich waters of Scotland's fourth largest freshwater loch. Broad Loch Ewe is also spectacular. At its southern end is Inverewe Garden, a horticultural surprise that captivates everyone, not just botanists. In 1862, Osgood MacKenzie, a gardener only 20 years old, created the gardens on a peninsula belonging to Inverewe House, laboriously draining a peat bog and enriching the soil with clay from the coast. Thus fertile soil was created on which lush subtropical vegetation thrives, aided by a mild climate tempered by the Atlantic gulf stream. The gardens were donated to the National Trust for Scotland in 1952. Covering about 20 ha (50 acres), they are open to the public all year round.

A view of Beinn Alligin (985 m/ 3,232 ft) (below, top) and Loch Shieldaig (below), with the Torridon Hills in the background. Glen Torridon is bounded by steep ridges of terraced Torridon sandstone (right). The Liathach massif seen from Loch Clair (centre right). Loch Shieldaig is fringed with forest (far right).

Torridon and Beinn Eighe Nature Reserve

Chains of lonely mountains, bizarre landscapes, lowering black forests and deep lochs – the mountain region around Torridon is a highlight of the Scottish Highlands. Most of the area is administered by the National Trust for Scotland. It lies north of Loch Shieldaig, which is fringed with magnificent forests of the native Scots pine; a small island in the loch is famed for its 19th-century stands of Scots pine and enjoys special protection. On the north shores of Upper Loch Torridon, you can stand and gaze in awe at Liathach and Beinn Alligin, Torridon sandstone peaks about 750 million years old; or you can climb them, provided you are fit, know the ropes and are professionally equipped. The Beinn Eighe Nature Reserve was designated Britain's first national nature reserve in 1951. Four nature trails wind through this beautiful region, known also for the diversity of its fauna.

Highland men traditionally wore tartan as a kilt and a plaid, over the shoulder. The pattern of squares and intersecting lines indicates clan affiliation (below). A bespoke kilt by a maker such as Ian Chisholm of Inverness (below right) attests to awareness of Scottish tradition. Accessories add a dash (right).

Clan MacLachlan

IN RIVALRY UNITED: THE SCOTTISH CLANS

Scottish society was traditionally structured into a ramified clan system. Feudal agrarian clan hierarchies developed from the original Celtic tribal system, fusing with the Norman feudal system in the high Middle Ages. A clan chief both commanded and protected aristocrats; as his vassals, they went into battle for him. The bottom tier consisted of clansmen bound to the aristocrats by ties of kinship and loyalty; they were farmers and herdsmen on lands that belonged by medieval law to the kings of Scotland, but were divided up and administered autonomously by the clans. Clan feuds seething below the surface often weakened royal armies. The end of the clan structure began in 1707, when Scotland and England were united; by the time the last Jacobite Rising was quelled in 1746, nothing was left of it. Great landowners evicted the Highland sustenance farmers from their arable lands in a forced displacement known by the emotionally charged term "Highland Clearances" – in the late 18th and early 19th centuries, some 60 per cent of Highlanders were expelled from their crofts and either emigrated to the New World or eked out a living in the coastal villages. However, the clan spirit lives on, as the prosperity of makers of bespoke tartan kilts such as Ian Chisholm (large picture right) attests.

In the summer months, a train pulled by a puffing steam engine (inset) runs from Fort William via the Glenfinnan Viaduct to Mallaig, past Loch Shiel with the evocative Glenfinnan Monument (below). Ferries to the Hebrides depart from Ullapool (right and far right) and Mallaig (centre right).

Scenic routes through the Highlands to the islands

Marvellous panoramic views make driving through the Highlands a spectacular sightseeing tour – a rather winding stretch runs westward from Fort William for about 72 km (45 miles), skirting mountains and lochs to Mallaig. About halfway between is Loch Shiel, a long body of water with the poignant Glenfinnan Monument at its northern end – the figure of a Highlander stands on a column close to the shore, marking the spot where Bonnie Prince Charlie gathered the clans against the English in August 1745. You can also reach Mallaig from Fort William on the nostalgic "Jacobite steam train", which runs from June to September. It featured in some scenes of the Harry Potter films, notably the second one, as the Hogwarts Express. A third scenic route is to drive from Invergarry, north-east of Fort William, through dramatic scenery to Ullapool.

The ruins of Urquhart Castle on a headland (below) are a tangible tourist attraction, unlike "Nessie", the Loch Ness Monster, imaginatively represented here. Nessie has been a protected species since 1934, and should anyone manage to catch this legendary saurian, it must be returned to the loch immediately.

LEGEND LIVES: THE LOCH NESS MONSTER

Loch Ness – a dark, freshwater loch 36 km (22 miles) long, average width 1.5 km (0.9 miles), up to 230 m (754 ft) deep and never warmer than 7°C (44° F) – sounds like the ideal habitat for the primordial monster known worldwide as "Nessie". It made its first appearance as long ago as 556, when the Irish missionary St Columba banished it again to the murky waters with the words "Thou shalt go no further. Go back with all speed!". Then the holy man made the sign of the Cross, which evidently so intimidated the monster that it stayed hidden for 1,000 years. In the 16th century, it resurfaced to devour three men, but was then not sighted again until 1933, when construction of the A82 along the north shore of the loch must have disturbed it. Since then, "encounters with the monster" have been frequent. Scientists have been seriously trying to prove that Nessie exists. One theory has it that Loch Ness was once linked with the sea but was cut off by glacier action, leaving a saurian trapped in the loch. In 1976, a team of American researchers concluded that "something must be living in the loch" – a vertebrate breathing through gills, of which between 30 and 50 individuals would have to be thriving in Loch Ness at all times in order to ensure the survival of the species over the millennia.

The Caledonian Canal (below) runs between Fort William and Inverness, linking the Atlantic with the North Sea. Fort Augustus (right) is a tiny village at the southern end of Loch Ness. It consists mainly of five locks that lift boats from the level of the large loch to that of the canal.

The Caledonian Canal

Many fans of Scotland have fulfilled the dream of navigating the Caledonian Canal under their own steam. Arguably Europe's most beautiful waterway, the canal links the Atlantic with the North Sea via Fort William and Inverness. Some 100 km (62 miles) long, 6 m (19.6 ft) deep and up to 30 m (33 yds) across, the canal, which opened in 1922, flows through diverse scenery. Fitted with numerous locks, the canal begins in the south with a fjord, Loch Linnhe, then crosses the inland basins Loch Lochy, Loch Oich and Loch Ness and flows into the Moray Firth. Today, only a few freighters use the canal but houseboat traffic has increased considerably – after a thorough introductory course with a film on how to pilot a houseboat, you are ready to start off. The houseboat-hire firm provides life jackets, charts and provisions for this panoramic voyage.

Lake Morlich (below) is encircled by the truly spectacular Cairngorms (Gaelic: "Blue Hills") (right). Heaven for hill-walkers and winter sports enthusiasts, the region is studded with 49 "Munros" – the Scottish term for mountains over 914 m (3,000 ft) high.

The Cairngorm Mountains

The rugged Highlands provide unbroken solitude in many places, such as at Loch Morlich in the Cairngorms National Park. Water sports aficionados are especially drawn to this spot. The red granite massif is part of the Grampians stretching south-east of the Great Glen and rising to heights of up to 1,300 m (4,266 ft). The topography of the Cairngorms is predominantly alpine. Numerous troughs, often with lakes at the bottom, attest to the action of ice age glaciation. However, there are also softly rounded mountains and hills here. Mountain heathland and high moorland plateaux provide diverse scenery. In winter, the Cairngorms National Park is a popular skiing and winter sports area, concentrated in three resorts. Chairlifts overcome a difference of 700 m (2,297 ft) in altitude and some 40 km (25 miles) of pistes are available for skiing.

Apart from Highland dancing performed by kilt-clad dancers and accompanied by bagpipes, spectators at the Highland Games marvel at the stone put, weight throw and tug of war (below left). The Queen is a guest at the Braemar Royal Highland Gathering on the first weekend in September (below and right).

FESTIVITIES OF A SPECIAL KIND: HIGHLAND GAMES

The Scots, well known for their hospitality and general friendliness, also have a pronounced predilection for staging bizarre events! The Highland Games, held between May and September at some 100 venues all over Scotland, are a good example of this. It is not known when the games originated, although they are believed to have fea-tured at village festivals. However, notably bellicose elements suggest that the tradition must go back at least to the days of clan feuding. Following a renaissance in the 19th century, the games developed into a sort of Highland Olympics, drawing a Scottish public as well as tourists. Heavy disciplines such as the stone put, the Scottish hammer throw and the caber toss are guaranteed crowd-pleasers. It's not always easy to work out the point of some disciplines – what counts in "tossing the caber", a tall pine pole, is not how far it goes but rather to ensure that the caber turns end over end to hit the ground at "12 o'clock" relative to the direction of the run that launched the toss. The first official Highland Games were staged at Braemar in 1832. After the young Queen Victoria first attended the "Braemar Highland Gathering" in 1848 and threw her weight behind reviving the custom, Highland Games began to feature regularly on the Scottish calendar of events – and still do.

Sunrise over Loch Rannoch (below). Beyond the western shore of the loch, boggy Rannoch Moor, which is dotted with ponds, stretches all the way to Glen Coe, Britain's largest tract of moorland. In sleepy fishing villages such as Pennan on the north-east coast (inset), life passes much more slowly. Cinema aficionados will probably recognise Pennan from the film "Local Hero" with Burt Lancaster.

THE NORTH-EAST

Keeps, castles and whisky distilleries – awareness of history and a comfortable way of life are expressed distinctively in north-east Scotland, which is altogether a gentler part of the country. You can sense this from the number of castle trails and whisky trails that are there for the taking. The scenery tends to be tranquil with panoramic vistas of peat bogs and fertile meadows, stands of birch and fir, small fishing villages, and larger settlements and farms the further east you go.

The best view of Dunrobin Castle, with its towers and "pepperpots" (right), is from the garden (below). Left, from top: hunting trophies; the Robe Room; the dining room; the Green and Gold Room (a bedroom); the Seamstress Room, with the family insignia.

Dunrobin Castle

The earls of Sutherland were among the most powerful landowners in Europe when they had Dunrobin Castle built on the site of an early medieval fort near the small village of Golspie. Now grandly "Scottish Baronial" in style, Dunrobin is set on a natural terrace high above the sea. Surrounded by a large park, the seat of the Sutherlands has a total of 189 rooms. The earliest parts of the building, which looks most impressive when viewed from the garden side, date from the late 13th century. The towers and "pepperpots" that have sprouted in the course of renovations are typical of Victorian castle architecture. The imposing façade does not fool many Scots, who associate Dunrobin Castle with a dark side of Scottish history – the earls of Sutherland were among the landowners most active in promoting the Highland Clearances.

Past and present: In front of Inverness Castle (below) is a statue commemorating Flora MacDonald (right), who saved Charles Stuart (Bonnie Prince Charlie), the Young Pretender. The High Street (far right) is a popular place to shop. There were once 30 clan villages on Loch Rannoch (inset).

Inverness

The roots of the city of Inverness, today a modern administrative seat, go deep – back to the times of the Picts, the "Painted Ones". "Picti" was the Roman name for the pre-Celtic and Celtic tribes in Scotland, north of the Antonine Wall between the Firth of Forth and the Firth of Clyde, who resisted the Romans so vigorously from the late 3rd century AD. St Columba is said to have converted Bridei (Bruide), king of the Picts, to Christ- ianity here in the 6th century. Inverness Castle, a 19th- century edifice, looms over the city and is now an office building of feudal grandeur housing the local adminis- tration. Legend has it that Macbeth murdered King Dun- can, the rightful heir to the throne of Scotland, at his fort to the east of Inverness Castle. In 1746, the last, decisive battle was fought between England and Scotland at Culloden, not far from the city centre.

It takes five years to learn the highly specialised craft of pipe making, which is often handed down from generation to generation. Right: Pipe maker Alan Logan and a colleague in the workshop. Opposite: Logan with a finished instrument (above) and a pipe band in the High Street, Inverness (below).

BAGPIPES: A SYMBOL OF SCOTTISH IDENTITY

For many, bagpipes are associated with "Scottishness". Brought to Britain by the Romans, pipes originated as the classic herdsman's instrument in Asia and North Africa. The air needed to blow the instrument is constantly introduced to the bag (made of sheep- or seal-skin) through a blowpipe or, in the case of "coldpipes", through a bellows. Attached to the bag are the chanter or melody pipe (there is also a two-pipe chanter), which is bored for fingering, and two to three continually sounding "drones" (pitched one or two octaves below the chanter or consonant with the fifth of the chanter). The player's upper arm presses the air from the bag into the drones. Such is the Scottish passion for the "pipes" that they came to symbolise Scottish identity and were suppressed by the English following the Union. It is said that a piper academy was founded in the 15th century on Skye in the Inner Hebrides by the MacCrimmons, pipers to the Clan MacLeod. Players of the Great Highland Bagpipe know hundreds of "pibroch" melodies, including laments for the dead and marches, as well as music for Highland dancing – "reels" and "strathspeys" (stately dances). By the Victorian era, the bagpipes were accompanying Highland regiments abroad as a morale booster for those engaged in building the Empire.

The mountains in beautiful Glen Affric are almost alpine. The valley with its ancient pine woods in a Caledonian Forest Reserve is embraced by the arms of deep blue Loch Affric (below, right and far right). Loch Beinn a' Mheadhoin (centre right) is startlingly clear.

Glen Affric

Glen Affric, part of the ancient Caledonian Forest near the city of Inverness, is often described as Scotland's most beautiful glen. Its many fans love it for its pine woods. Here, in this valley so richly forested in Scots pine, it is possible to experience just how many shades of green there are in nature. A walk through the forests and hills on a lovely autumn day can be both invigorating and restful. Start your walk through this scenic region in the village of Cannich, where three glens and a strath (wide valley) meet – Strathglass, Cannich, Urquhart and Affric. A small wooden suspension bridge spans the River Affric. A long trail takes you to waterfalls, ruins and mountain vistas, but this is a strenuous undertaking and should be well planned. Adventure holiday addicts (and romantics) gather at the Glen Affric Youth Hostel on a remote peninsula.

The North East Coastal Trail (right) runs from Fraserburgh via Portgordon to sleepy fishing villages such as Pennan and Crovie (below). Inset, left to right: a medieval cross in Banff; Duff House, designed by the Scottish architect William Adam; the lighthouse at the entrance to Macduff Port.

Banff and Macduff

Picturesque fishing villages along the North Sea coast, such as Crovie, often consist of no more than a couple of terraces – but are enchanting to look at. Banff and Macduff, astride the mouth of the River Deveron, are linked by a bridge (1799) with seven arches. Banff was a hub of the Hanseatic League in the 12th century. The listed Georgian houses built by the Scottish gentry, who discovered the attractions of this idyllic spot in the 17th and 18th centuries, are well worth a visit. Although unfinished, Duff House exemplifies classic Georgian architecture. Designed by William Adam, the paramount influence on the Scottish architecture of the period, Duff House was inspired by the Roman Villa Borghese. In an entirely different vein, the Macduff Marine Aquarium is home to more than 50 species of fish, which normally only scuba divers are able to see so close up.

Fiercely fought over, then forgotten –
Oliver Cromwell besieged Dunottar
Castle for eight months in 1651/2 in
order to capture the Scottish royal
insignia. When at last the castle sur-
rendered, he was forced to accept
that they had long since been
smuggled out of harm's way.

Dunottar Castle

The ruins of the keep, set against the grand backdrop of a rocky coast near the small harbour of Stonehaven, are so stunningly beautiful that Dunottar Castle might be taken for the product of a talented stage designer's imagination. If you need to convince yourself that this mighty fortress in Aberdeenshire is genuine, you can do so all year round (but from November to Easter only until dusk, which falls early). The castle stands on a 50-m (164-ft) high hill, which drops off precipitously. St Ninian is said to have founded a Christian settlement here in the 5th century. Early in the 14th century, Sir William Keith discovered the strategic advantages of this location for realising his military ambitions and built "Dunotir", which was later extensively enlarged. Damaged by Cromwell's forces and abandoned in 1715, the old keep has slowly fallen into decay.

The barley is steeped, left to germinate then kiln-dried (below). Right
and far right: Distilleries on the
"Whisky Trail". Centre right: Wood
casks in Dufftown. Left, from top:
Coopers in a workshop; barley on the
Orkneys; a malting vat. Opposite:
Years of slow maturing in the cask
guarantee a memorable first sip.

WHISKY: BOTTLED SUNLIGHT

The calm, dedication and authority with which the Scots set about the process of producing their national drink seems to flow directly into the bottles. In the 6th century, Irish monks (as a sideline while converting the heathen) began to distil fiery beverages – the distillation of whisky in Scotland is first recorded in 1494. To produce Scotch, dried barley is cleaned, soaked for two or three days in water in a steep then left to germinate in a malting vat. Peat can be burnt below the grain bed, which is equipped with small holes, to smoke the malt and give it a distinctive aroma. The malt is milled into grist then mixed with hot water in the mash tun. The wort is pumped into large vats called "wash backs" and yeast is added to initiate fermentation. In distillation, the copper onion-shaped pot stills are heated to a high temperature; Scottish distilleries usually distil twice. The second distillation produces the "middle cut" to be matured in casks. Leaving "bottled sunlight" to mature in oak casks for at least three years allows the distillate to develop its colour and taste. There are three types of cask: the butt (500 ltr/132 gal), the hogshead (254 ltr/67 gal) and the standard barrel (190 ltr/50 gal). Filtered into large vats, natural substances are sometimes added to give depth to the whisky hues.

View of the harbour and skyline, where new and old come together (below). Marischal College (right) is part of the University of Aberdeen; a figure above a bank building in Union Street (centre right); Aberdeen's seaport is deep enough to handle ocean-going vessels (far right).

Aberdeen

Aberdeen, situated between the Rivers Dee and Don, is often called "the granite city" because most of its buildings are made of stone quarried from the hinterland. This historic city in the Grampians (population some 212,000) is Scotland's third largest. It was once described by the Scottish king Alexander I, who reigned from 1107 to 1124, as the most important city in his kingdom. Even then it was a major trading centre with a fishing harbour. In 1337, "Aberdon", as it was then called, was burnt to the ground by the English king Edward III (reigned 1327 to 1377). Commercial and trading activity again brought the city prosperity and renown in the succeeding centuries; then, in the mid-20th century, oil was discovered in the North Sea. Now known as "the oil capital of Europe", Aberdeen is a major service harbour serving the offshore oil rigs.

The earliest parts of Blair Castle near Pitlochry date from the 13th century. Thirty rooms are open to the public (below, clockwise from top left: the drawing room, the stairwell, the arsenal and the Red Bedchamber). Balmoral Castle (right) is the summer residence of the British Royal Family.

KEEPS AND CASTLES: HISTORY EVERYWHERE YOU LOOK

Glamour and the glories of generations long past, riches and power from the top of the tower to the dungeon – where else is history so spine-tinglingly alive as in the 3,000 keeps and castles with which Scotland so obligingly delights its visitors? There is a distinction between keeps or donjons that evolved over the centuries into "fortified habitations", such as Kildrummy Castle (now ruined), and the simple fortified tower houses built by lairds (owner of a landed estate) on their lands – the early part of Drum Castle, dating from the 13th and 14th centuries, is an early tower house. From the mid-16th century, manor houses succeeded the tower houses – matching the tastes dictated by the English rulers of the time, they were either in the Elizabethan or Jacobean style, or (when commissioned by men from the lower ranks of the aristocracy) in the Scottish Baronial style (such as Craigievar Castle). The fantastic façades and magnificent staterooms in castles that belonged to the nobility or to kings are often in Italian palazzo style. The Aberdeen hinterland, "Royal Deeside", abounds in such relics of past grandeur. Head for the Castle Trail – this spectacular route visits eleven fortified habitations, fairy-tale castles and grand manor houses with towers and fortifications to suit every taste.

John Ruskin (1819–1900), writer, social reformer and art critic, wrote of Dunblane Cathedral, consecrated in 1228: "I know of nothing so perfect in its simplicity, and so beautiful in all Gothic…" (below).

"The Malt Shovel" pub (inset) is at the lower end of Cockburn Street in Edinburgh, on the way into the Old Town. Now, what would be the favourite drink served to regulars frequenting a pub with this name?

PERTHSHIRE, ANGUS AND DUNDEE, THE KINGDOM OF FIFE

Going south to Perthshire, into the old heart of Scotland with the bordering counties of Angus and Dundee, you find a region that is mountainous in the north and west, agricultural, and rather thinly settled. The south and east, on the other hand, are more densely populated – Dundee, Scotland's fourth largest city, grew into the world's leading jute-processing centre in the 19th century. Golfers in particular are drawn to the Kingdom of Fife, a beautiful peninsula between the Firth of Tay and the Firth of Forth.

Most of Glamis Castle (right and below) was built in the second half of the 17th century. The Earls of Strathmore, forebears of the late Queen Mother, built a fortified habitation here a thousand years before. A visit to Glamis includes a peek at the "Queen Mum's" childhood bedroom.

Glamis Castle

North of Dundee is a gem of a romantic Scottish castle with all the trimmings – the turrets, crenellations and "pepperpots" are typical of the Scottish Baronial style. A distinguishing feature of this style is that the architectural elements that were once essential for defence are used as ornament without function. William Shakespeare chose Glamis Castle as the setting for his tragic history play "Macbeth", allegedly to flatter King James I of England (VI of Scotland). The historical person Macbeth actually killed Duncan I, King of Scotland, in battle near Elgin and succeeded him as king of Scotland in 1040. The delightful Glamis Castle grounds were laid out in 1770 by the distinguished English landscape gardener Lancelot "Capability" Brown. The late Princess Margaret, sister to Queen Elizabeth II, was born in the "Queen Mum's" bedroom at Glamis.

St Andrews Cathedral (below), built in the 12th century and now in ruins, was once Scotland's largest church building. The Fife Peninsula has idyllic scenery – Crail, at the tip of the peninsula (right); the lighthouse at Elie (centre right); Pittenweem port (far right).

The Kingdom of Fife

Separated from the city of Edinburgh by the broad expanse of the Firth of Forth, the Kingdom of Fife is located on a wide bay in the central heartland of Scotland. Its name, which is still in common use, goes back to the days of the Picts (see page 79), when Fife was an independent kingdom. Hilly arable land and small fishing villages make this region very easy on the eye. The largest town on the peninsula is Kirkcaldy; since 1975 the administrative centre for Fife has been the new town of Glenrothes, which became a magnet for high-tech start-ups, particularly in semiconductors – the surrounding region is called "Silicon Glen". The past has also been lovingly nurtured here. Historic Culross, on the Firth of Forth, is notable for its crow-stepped buildings dating from the 17th and 18th centuries, when trade with the Lowlands flourished.

St Andrews is the home of golf (right and inset). The clubhouse of the Royal and Ancient Golf Club of St Andrews is near the old stone bridge at the 18th hole of the Old Course (below). Books on golf and St Andrews simply name "Mother Nature" as the landscape architect of this legendary course.

ST ANDREWS: WHERE GOLFING DREAMS COME TRUE

According to Sir Walter Simpson, the 19th-century Scottish authority on golf history, shepherds – obviously Scottish shepherds – were the founding fathers of the sport. They started out by hitting stones ahead of them with their crooks, just to pass the time; but the whole thing grew into a sport, with the aim of driving the stones into prescribed goals – rabbit holes. This may be just one of the many legends that have sprung up around golf, but here at St Andrews it sounds particularly plausible. The golf metropolis on the east coast of Scotland is home to the world's most famous golf club. Golf was presumably played at St Andrews long before 1553, the date mentioned in the first records of the sport there. The Society of St Andrews Golfers was established in 1754 and in 1834 the club was granted the designation "Royal". The clubhouse, ensconced high above the links, was built in 1854. The Open Championship, known in the US as the British Open, takes place here every two years, drawing players from all over the world to St Andrews. bishop Henry Wardlaw founded Scotland's first institute of higher learning here in 1410. The British Golf Museum, across from the clubhouse, is entertainingly informative for anyone interested in the history of golf – in Scottish shepherds, crooks and rabbit holes…

Lismore Island, in Loch Linnhe, north-west of Oban, is 14 km (9 miles) long and only 2.5 km (1.5 miles) wide (inset). The lighthouse is located at the southern tip at the entrance to the Sound of Mull. North of Glasgow lies

Loch Lomond, said to be the most beautiful loch in Scotland. Forming part of the Loch Lomond and the Trossachs National Park, it is set in a characteristic wild and romantic Highland landscape.

THE WESTERN HIGHLANDS AND THE ISLANDS

Clan chieftains were as ready to seize the most beautiful places in the Western Highlands as they were elsewhere, and had no qualms about taking existing settlements. The tower houses and castles of the Stewarts, MacDonalds and Campbells tell tales of fierce battles fought over land and turbulent family histories down through the centuries. Rugged mountains, deep blue lochs, steep cliffs and craggy coasts – where the fisherman's trade is still pursued in many places – evoke the quintessential Scottish atmosphere.

Oban has grown into a busy port town (below and right). High above the town, MacCaig's Tower is a replica of the Colosseum in Rome (far right). It was built in the late 19th century, commissioned by John Stuart MacCaig, a philanthropic banker who wanted to combat unemployment by creating jobs.

Spirit of Fairbr

Oban

Back in the 19th century, the small town of Oban on the west coast of Scotland was just one of many fishing villages. However, with the advent of the steamship and the beginnings of rail travel – the railway line was built in 1880 – Oban grew into a major fishing and ferry harbour, with ferry services steadily increasing. Now, Oban is "the gateway to the Western Isles". Ferries ply between the harbour and the islands of Mull, Coll, Tiree, South Uist, Barra and so on; in addition, there are day trips to Staffa and Iona. An appealing town with a population of around 8,000, Oban is also popular because of its ideal situation on a sheltered bay with the island of Kerrera offshore. Sailing, swimming and hill-walking (the Grampian Mountains are not far away) make a stay here well worthwhile. Before setting out for the islands, be sure to take a stroll through the pretty harbour.

Castle Stalker (below, top). Once symbolic of clan power, the eerie ruins of Kilchurn Castle stand defiantly guarding Loch Awe (below and right). Sir Colin Campbell of Glenorchy had the keep built around 1450 and fortification walls were added in 1693.

Stalker Castle and Kilchurn Castle

Solitary, doughty, the stuff of legend – Castle Stalker stands on a small island in Loch Linnhe, just off the coast at Oban. Still privately owned, this four-storey tower house looks back on a turbulent history. Clan chief Sir John Stewart is thought to have had it built in the mid-15th century for his illegitimate son, whose mother he intended to marry to ensure that the line continued. Sir John Stewart lived just long enough to marry before dying from the after-effects of an assault made on him during the festivities – the family took revenge in battle. The tower house continued to be hotly contested and it was eventually abandoned in 1840. In 1965, Lt Colonel Stewart Allward bought it and spent ten years carefully restoring the house. In contrast, the proud ruins of Kilchurn Castle, on a peninsula jutting out into Loch Awe between Oban and Inverary, look haunting and lonely.

Inveraray is on the wooded shores of Loch Fyne (right). The town's main attraction is the eclectic Revival-style Inveraray Castle (below; inset: entrance hall and salon); begun in 1746, this fabulous castle, designed for the Duke of Argyll by architects including Sir John Vanbrugh and Roger Morris, was finished in 1789.

Inveraray

A narrow bridge leads to the small, picturesque town of Inveraray on Loch Fyne. Lovingly restored Highland houses in the narrow streets recall everyday life in the heyday of the clans. This is a place where it is well worth spending some "quality museum time". Prison cells, inmate biographies, court records and medieval torture instruments are on display at the old courthouse – an exciting excursion back into several centuries of Scottish criminology. Set in an enchanting park with woods and lawns, Inverary Castle was built in Revival style by some very distinguished architects in the 18th century, on the foundations of a medieval fort. The castle, which features corner turrets, conical roofs and emphatic neo-Gothic crenellation, is home to the Dukes of Argyll, heads of the ancient Clan Campbell, who moved here from Loch Awe in the early 15th century.

The wild salmon population has declined markedly but there is still a good chance of landing the king of fish – and a trusty labrador at your side helps to while away hours spent on the banks of a stream waiting for the salmon to rise. Salmon is hung up for smoking in large commercial "smoke houses".

SALMON FARMING AND ANGLING IN SCOTLAND

Scotland's waters, both freshwater and salt, teem with herring, cod (in steep decline), mackerel, sole, trout and salmon, lobster and mussels. Boats from Scottish fishing harbours are responsible for more than two thirds of the fish caught in British waters. However, fishing – once a pillar of the Scottish economy – is in the throes of a serious crisis. In many coastal areas, aquaculture has recently caught on, although environmental objections, such as disease transfer and cross-breeding with the wild salmon population, continue to be raised. In western Scotland and the Inner Hebrides, salmon farming has become a major industry. The cultured salmon yield grew from fewer than 1,000 tonnes (1,102 tons) in the early 1970s to 15,000 tonnes (16,534 tons) by the mid-1990s. Today, Scotland is the world's leading producer of cultured salmon. Trout and wild salmon are still abundant in rivers such as the Tweed and the Tay – some 10,000 salmon are caught by fly-fishermen annually in the River Spey. With more than 6,000 fresh-water and saltwater lochs, Scotland is heaven for anglers. Freshwater lochs are home to brown trout and rainbow trout, pike and many other sporting fish. The laws are strict about poaching in private waters but there are plenty of opportunities for visitors to angle with a fishing licence.

Stirling Castle sits in a strategically sound position on top of an extinct volcano (below). Waxwork figures in the castle (right) depict vanished eras, as do the carved oak portrait roundels known as the Stirling Heads (inset), which were once mounted on the ceiling of the King's Presence Chamber.

Stirling

Residents of Stirling (population 35,000) call their city the "Gateway to Scotland". Because of its strategic location, Stirling was always in the thick of things in Scottish history – in 1297, the Scots defeated the English at Stirling Bridge; in 1314, Robert the Bruce routed Edward II at nearby Bannockburn. The main attraction of the city, which has a modern university, is Stirling Castle, perched on a 76-m (349-ft) volcanic crag. The north German novelist Theodor Fontane waxed lyrical about the views: 'looking down into this county … one took home the loveliest view of any place that the Scottish landscape can grant.' The old town below the castle is also attractive. From the 13th century, Stirling was a prosperous centre for trade; later, it had its own mint – in 1538, under James V, sixpenny coins of base metal and 25 per cent silver were struck here, called "bawbees".

A castle, a palace, a volcano (extinct), more restaurants per capita than London and five different festivals in August alone – no wonder Edinburgh tops the polls year after year as Britain's best-loved city (below). For fun, take a "Witchery Tour" (inset) – the guide might pass himself off as a "hanged highwayman" come back from the dead just to take you through his old haunts…

EDINBURGH AND THE LOTHIANS

The Lothians – the region to the east and west of Edinburgh – could be called "the Scottish Lowlands". This area is bounded in the south by the Pentland Hills, and in the north by the Firth of Forth – from the economic standpoint, the most important estuary on the east coast of Scotland. For over five centuries, Edinburgh has been the cultural hub of Scotland. Like ancient Rome, the city was built on "seven hills" and has been called the "Athens of the North" since it was a stronghold of the Enlightenment in Britain.

Edinburgh's Grassmarket (below left) and Old Town (below right). Combine window-shopping in elegant Princes Street (right) with a relaxing pub crawl (far right). Until 2005, Jenners (centre right) was "the world's oldest independent department store". Inset: the King's Dining Room in the castle.

Edinburgh

In 1995, the Old and New Towns of Edinburgh were designated UNESCO World Cultural Heritage Sites. The architecture of the medieval Old Town contrasts sharply with the Georgian buildings of the New Town, planned on a grid layout in the late 18th century. Part of the massive Edinburgh Castle dates from the 11th century; St Margaret's Chapel, also on Castle Rock, was consecrated in 1090. Lawnmarket, High Street and Canongate form the Royal Mile, the main Old Town thoroughfare, with its labyrinth of closes and courtyards. Here, Gladstone's Land, a 17th-century merchant's house, rubs shoulders with sacred buildings, including late-Gothic St Giles' Cathedral, the Protestant High Kirk of Edinburgh. At the eastern end of the Royal Mile, next to a ruined Augustinian abbey built in 1128, is the Palace of Holyroodhouse, the seat of the kings of Scotland.

The Pipes & Drums perform the Military Tattoo on the Esplanade in front of Edinburgh Castle (below), part of the annual Edinburgh Festival. At the renowned alternative Fringe Festival (right), more than 10,000 artists of all kinds stage or perform in some 1,500 shows at more than 200 venues.

IT'S SHOWTIME: FESTIVAL CAPITAL EDINBURGH

Edinburgh is a magnet for artists all year round because no other city in the world provides quite such fertile cultural soil for the visual arts, music and, of course, the performing arts. August is the high point of the year – the renowned Edinburgh Festival is the world's largest and best festival of the performing arts, drawing at least two million visitors annually. Acrobats and jugglers invade the narrow streets, theatre groups turn the smallest of courtyards and closes into creative experimental stages, international music stars perform, cabaret, concerts, circuses, operas, films and ballet are featured. World-class art exhibitions round off this mind-boggling calendar of events. This glorious showmanship for all and sundry is underscored by the insistent drone of the pipes – some played by exhibitionist one-man bands, who have been practising all year for the great event, while the Pipes & Drums play the Military Tattoo on the Castle Esplanade for three weeks against the dramatic backdrop of the illuminated castle. The fabulous Edinburgh cultural summer starts in late July with the International Blues and Jazz Festival, followed by the Fringe Festival, famous the world over as the alternative to the establishment International Festival, which begins in mid-August and is host to more than 21,000 events.

Myths and legends – to the annoyance of scholars worldwide, Dan Brown has the Knights Templar hiding the Holy Grail in Rosslyn Chapel. A stone carving of maize that predates Columbus and allegorical representations such as the Dance of Death are further enigmas here.

Rosslyn Chapel

Roslin, south of Edinburgh, was once no more than a miners' settlement; but it possesses a now world-famous treasure – Rosslyn Chapel. This small church features prominently in Dan Brown's best-selling book (and subsequent film) "The Da Vinci Code", and as a result is saturated in myth. Around 1450, William Sinclair, 1st Earl of Caithness, endowed the chapel but it was left unfinished at his death in 1484. Only 21 m (69 ft) long, it was elaborately decorated by its architect and master masons and filled with works of allegorical sculpture that still perplex scholars today. One of the more conventional of the many legends associated with this place is that the late-Gothic Prentice Pillar, a sumptuously decorated column, really was made by an apprentice, who was struck dead for his pains by an envious master mason.

It's all in the name: The Pitcher & Piano Bar and the Drum & Monkey, both in Glasgow (below, top left and centre); Deacon Brodie's Tavern (below, top right and bottom centre), Bannerman's Pub (below, bottom left), Abbotsford Bar (below, bottom right), The Filling Station (right) and The Griffin (far right), all in Edinburgh.

THE FILLING STATION

PUBS: SCOTTISH HOSPITALITY AND CONVIVIALITY

Taking a break in one of the innumerable typical Scottish pubs is not just refreshing – it's also a good opportunity to see genuine Scottish hospitality and sociability at work. Many pubs now incorporate restaurants; the range of culinary delights runs from sandwiches to juicy Black Angus steaks served with chips, or haggis, a traditional concoction of ground sheep's heart, lungs and liver cooked in a natural casing (the sheep's stomach), which tastes much better than it sounds. The British public house was invented in the Victorian era – in 1915, closing time was regulated by law at 11 pm to prevent workmen from drinking to the small hours and turning up at the factory with a nasty (and unproductive) hangover. Landlords rang a bell and shouted "Last orders!" at 10.45 pm. Customers had to gulp down as much as possible by 11 pm ("Drink up please!") – often imbibing too much in record time, which is said to have lead to the modern problem of binge drinking. The regulations have been relaxed but the jury is still out on whether the desired results have been achieved. The no-smoking law now in effect has brought more people to pubs but publicans are making less money. Edinburgh pubs tend to stay open to 1 am but many are open much longer – a chance to get in one last round of darts.

The welcoming Albert Hotel in North Queensferry (below), with the Forth Rail Bridge in the background. The engineers Sir John Fowler and Sir Benjamin Baker built the bridge (2.5 km/1.5 miles long) over the Firth of Forth between 1883 and 1890 to carry the railway line running north from Edinburgh.

Firth of Forth

The Firth of Forth at Edinburgh separates the Kingdom of Fife to the north from the Lothians in the south. Between North Queensferry and South Queensferry the estuary is crossed by the Forth Rail Bridge and the Forth Road Bridge. Where ferries had plied for centuries, a marvel of 19th-century engineering was completed in 1890 – the Forth Rail Bridge, 2.5 km (1.5 miles) long and painted bright red. Then the world's longest bridge, the boldly curving cantilevered structure has remained a benchmark of engineering in Scotland and has been nominated for UNESCO World Cultural Heritage status. Trains cross it 50 m (164 ft) above the water, permitting ships to pass beneath, and it has taken modern rail traffic in its stride. A supreme example of bridge building that has not become outdated, it was joined by a toll bridge for motor vehicles in 1964.

The tragic heroine Mary Queen of Scots was born at Linlithgow Palace in the Lothians (below and inset). Her ill-chosen array of lovers and husbands cost the queen the affection of her Scottish subjects. The dining room (right), bedchamber (far right) and Mary's death mask at Lennoxlove House in Haddington.

MARY STUART AND ELIZABETH I

The story of Queen Elizabeth I and Mary Queen of Scots, two powerful women who for decades were rivals for the English throne, is world-famous. Mary Queen of Scots has inspired works of literature both fictional – such as Madame de La Fayette's "La Princesse de Clèves" (1678) and Sir Walter Scott's "The Abbot" (1820) – and non-fictional, including Antonia Fraser's highly acclaimed biography (1969). Born in 1542, Mary Stuart was the daughter of James V of Scotland and his French wife, Marie de Guise. At the age of nine months she was crowned Queen of Scots on her father's death. At fifteen, she was married to the French dauphin but he soon died and she returned to Scotland as a dangerous rival to Elizabeth I, the Virgin Queen. Taken into custody by the English, the beautiful and, like her rival, highly educated Mary Stuart became a tragic pawn in the contest between the Catholic and Protestant factions. She languished in prison for some eighteen years since Elizabeth I could not quite bring herself to authorise Mary's execution, despite the threat that she re-presented. However, accusations of intrigues initiated by Mary against Elizabeth finally induced the English queen to sign the death warrant – very reluctantly – and Mary was doomed. She was beheaded on February 8, 1587.

Once disparaged as dingy, Glasgow is now a modern cultural metropolis and hub of the service industry; successful restructuring has compensated for the decline of heavy industry and shipbuilding.

The spectacular Clyde Auditorium (below) is an elegant Glasgow events and concert venue, built by Foster and Partners on the River Clyde. "The Armadillo" has reconfigured the dockside skyline.

GLASGOW AND THE CLYDE VALLEY

From the Lead Hills, the lovely Clyde Valley winds towards the sea through fertile Lanarkshire to reach the city of Glasgow, once the industrial capital of the British Empire. The valley unites pristine countryside with market gardens, garden centres and industrial facilities, which have all prospered with the help of hydroelectric power and a favourable coastal location. The Clyde estuary flows into the Atlantic on the west coast and made transatlantic shipping possible from an early date.

Glasgow past and present. (Right) The Burrell Collection, Pollok Country Park; the Modern Art Gallery; the Glasgow School of Art library. (Below left, from top) The Town Hall; the Moses window and crypt, Glasgow Cathedral. (Below right, top) The Modern Art Gallery; the Glasgow Science Centre. (Below right, bottom) The cathedral nave. Opposite page: (Left, from top) The People's Palace; the Horse Shoe pub; Port Glasgow.

Glasgow and Port Glasgow

Designated the European Capital of Culture in 1990 and the UK City of Architecture and Design in 1999, Glasgow is Scotland's biggest city, with a population of some 600,000. The city no longer hides its light under a bushel but greets visitors with exclusive shops, grand façades and attractive shopping malls right at the centre of the city. Glasgow exudes cosmopolitan flair and the radical change in the city's image in the past two decades has led to talk of it being much trendier than Edinburgh, its arch-rival. A record number of theatres and other cultural venues, world-class art museums and more than 70 parks and green zones have lifted the face of a city that was once notorious for dilapidated buildings and the unattractive public housing in the Gorbals. Port Glasgow with its dockyards and historic Newark Castle (16th century) is about 40 km (25 miles) to the west.

The Willow Tea Room, Sauchiehall Street (right). The Mackintosh House, where he lived, rebuilt in the Hunterian Art Gallery complex (main picture and below left: first, second and fourth picture). Glasgow School of Art (below left, third picture). Below, far right: Hill House, designed for the publisher Walter Blackie.

MACKINTOSH: SCOTTISH ART NOUVEAU

Glasgow's standing as a design metropolis goes back to the late 19th century – with their distinctive interpretation of Art Nouveau, "The Four" (Mackintosh, his wife Margaret MacDonald, her sister Frances and Herbert MacNair, who married Frances) were avant-garde and soon became famous throughout Europe. Their co-founder and head, Charles Rennie Mackintosh (1868–1928), was one of a policeman's eleven children, fortunate indeed in being able to follow his talent and inclinations – after training in an architectural practice, he took courses at the Glasgow Art Academy. Mackintosh designed houses, furniture and decorative fixtures and fittings. His unmistakable style unites functional simplicity with playful attention to mood-creating detail. Mackintosh's favourite shades – white, grey, pale olive and purple – are both cool and reassuringly gentle. The young designer became a modish architect in 1896 with his design for the Glasgow School of Art in Renfrew Street. Walter Gropius, German architect, industrial designer and Bauhaus founder, called it "the beginning of the breakthrough". World-famous in his lifetime, Charles Rennie Mackintosh had his own pavilion at the Secession exhibition in Vienna, and in 1902 his "Scottish Pavilion" was a hit at the Turin Exposition of Modern Design.

View of the Eildon Hills and the wooded valley of the River Tweed (below). Sir Walter Scott lived at Abbotsford House, near Melrose Abbey (inset: the library): "… while it pleases a fantastic person in the … manner of the architecture and decoration it has all the comforts of a commodious habitation." The writer's favourite spot, "Scott's View", is on a hilltop a few miles east of Melrose near Bemeryde.

THE SOUTH

The River Tweed, a great salmon river, flows through the south of Scotland, draining the Borders region, which is heavily wooded. Pastureland and moors lap at lonely hills. Along the North Sea coast from North Berwick via Dunbar to the border with England, steep cliffs alternate with idyllic coves and deserted sandy beaches. It was here that Scotland had to defend her borders from frequent English incursions – "the Scottish Borders" is not just an administrative unit, but also has emotional associations.

The interior of Culzean Castle matches its splendid exterior (main picture). Right: The Picture Room; the Oval Staircase; the apartment at the top, given to General Dwight D. Eisenhower by the Kennedys. Girvan (inset) is a pretty port town near Culzean Castle.

Culzean Castle and Girvan

High above the Ayrshire cliffs stands Culzean, one of Scotland's most magnificent castles. The 14th-century keep was enlarged to an L-shaped building under the supervision of renowned Scottish architect and interior designer Robert Adam between 1777 and his death in 1792. Its owners, the Kennedys, donated it to the National Trust for Scotland in 1945, stipulating that rooms should be given to General Eisenhower during his lifetime in recognition of his services to Scotland and Europe as Supreme Allied Commander, Europe, during World War II. To the south, Girvan is a pleasant seaside resort that hosts a late-summer international jazz festival. From there, a boat goes to Ailsa Craig (Gaelic "Creag Ealasaid: Elspeth's Rock"), an island bird sanctuary 16 km (10 miles) offshore, whose name commemorates yet another sad Scottish legend.

The ruins of Sweetheart Abbey, founded by Dervorguilla of Galloway (below). Drumlanrig Castle in Galloway, the seat of Clan Douglas in the late 17th century (right: Drawing Room; Morning Room; stairwell). Caerlaverock Castle (inset), south-east of Dumfries.

Dumfries and Galloway

The region of Dumfries and Galloway is often called "Burns Country" because Robert Burns, the Scottish national poet, retired here to spend the last years of his short life. The Robert Burns Centre commemorates him. Hilly south-west Scotland is a rich cultural landscape with beautiful gardens and parks, ruined abbeys and – of course – numerous castles. Dumfries, the region's largest town with a population of around 32,000, looks back on a long tradition – it was officially given the rights of a royal burgh in 1186. A popular holiday resort, Dumfries is surrounded by five lochs. The region was popular in the 19th century for a different reason – the restrictive English marriage laws did not apply in Gretna Green, the last village on the Scottish side of the border, and both characters in novels and real-life lovers ran away to marry here without parental permission.

Glimpses of Sir Walter Scott's manor, Abbotsford House, near Melrose, built for him in 1812–14. The writer's desk (below); bust of Scott, the Dining Room and the Drawing Room (right). Pubs in Dumfries (opposite) recall the poet Robert Burns, who died young and was renowned for his amorous adventures.

WALTER SCOTT AND ROBERT BURNS

Robert Burns (1759–1796) made history in Scotland as the national poet, Walter Scott (1771–1832) became the best known Scottish novelist – between them, they not only enhanced Scottish patriotism but also projected a romantic image of Scotland abroad. Burns, son of a poor Ayrshire tenant farmer, was a freemason, political radical and proto-Romantic, whose precocious talent as the "Ploughman Poet" ensured his fame throughout Scotland. A passionate advocate of the Enlightenment, he wrote his poetry primarily in Scots, the Lowlands variety of English, and English that was only slightly dialectal. His romantic, melancholy ballads and large collection of songs are still sung today ("Red, red Rose" and especially "Auld Lang Syne"). Celebrated in some salons of literary Edinburgh, in others he was looked down on and he had no inclination to teach in the capital. Instead he moved to Dumfries, where he died young (at the age of 37) of what would now be called a streptococcus infection. Walter Scott, a native of Edinburgh, started out writing poetry and then wrote numerous lengthy historical novels based on 500 years of Scottish and English history. The only one still widely read today is "Ivanhoe", a classic of the genre. Created a baronet in 1818, Sir Walter Scott died at the age of 61.

Jedburgh Abbey (below). The library (right) and the owner, Catherine Maxwell Stuart (centre right), of Traquair House, a fortified mansion and Scotland's oldest continuously inhabited house. The trophies at Scott's Abbotsford House (far right). Dryburgh Abbey (inset, left); Melrose Abbey (inset, right).

The Borders

Just across the border from England, Britain becomes "Scott Country", as the region is also called – you hear it in the dialect. The lovely hilly scenery along the River Tweed is home to tweed factories. Grand manor houses, some of them offering luxurious but surprisingly affordable overnight accommodation, and castles open to the public invite you to take impressive sightseeing tours. The Scottish Borders, now an administrative unit, look back on a history of battles fought to defend Scotland against English invasion – ruins tell stirring tales of the Wars of Scottish Independence, fought in the Lowlands from the late 13th century to the early 14th. Four abbeys, all dating from the first half of the 12th century, also played a paramount role in the wars. They became significantly important both culturally and economically – even kings sometimes had to beg for credit.

Sheep seem to have colonized islands such as the Isle of Arran (below). Europe's biggest sheep auction is at Lairg in the Highlands (inset). Farmers hope their sheep will fetch good prices at auction. Campbell's Tweedhouse in Beauly (right) features tweed woven from Scottish wool.

SHEEP: MEEK SOULS, THICK WOOL

No wonder Dolly the cloned sheep was the work of Scottish scientists – you might think they were the primary form of life in Scotland. Soay, in the St Kilda archipelago in the North Atlantic, gives its name to the Soay sheep, probably the oldest surviving breed. These meek ruminants were once a major source of revenue for Scottish agriculture. Grass – so lush it squeaks when sheep tear at it in the rain – is plentiful in many parts of the Highlands and the islands; and sheep are superbly protected against storms and cold by their thick, greasy wool. Warm, stylish Scottish knitwear, popular the world over, put Scotland on the fashion map. A sheep product in need of an advertising boost, however, is haggis, a Scottish delicacy made from well-seasoned ground sheep offal and oatmeal boiled in a bag made from the sheep's stomach. It is traditionally served with whisky. Scotland still exports wool products but sheep-farming no longer pays – work-intensive shearing and processing and transport costs, as well as a competitive world market, have led to a steep decline in turnover. But sheep will never disappear from Scotland – lamb for Scotland's many gourmet restaurants, haggis for Burns Night celebrations and peerless Scottish knitwear will ensure their survival. Border collie dogs are also at home here.

Thunderclouds loom above Ben Nevis and the boats on Loch Eil (below). At 1,344 m (4,469 ft) above sea level, Ben Nevis is Britain's highest mountain. Kilt Rock (inset), which drops sheer into the sea, marking the end of the Trotternish Peninsula in north-east Skye, is aptly named – the brownish basalt cliffs really do resemble the tartan pattern on a meticulously pleated kilt.

ATLAS

Scotland takes up about a quarter of the main island of Great Britain. It includes the Orkney and Shetland islands in the North Sea as well as the Inner and Outer Hebrides to the west in the Atlantic. Mainland Scotland falls into the subalpine and high mountains of the Highlands in the north, to which the groups of smaller islands also belong; the centrally located flat to hilly lowlands are designated the Central Lowlands; and the Southern Uplands to the south range from hilly to mountainous.

Scotland, a scenic wonderland: renowned for its wildness, the valley of Glencoe is popular for winter sports, walking and climbing. Some peaks, such as Buachaille Etive Mór (1,022 m/3,353 ft) shown here are over 1,000 m (3,280 ft) above sea level.

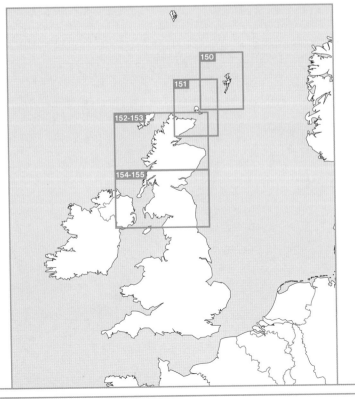

MAP KEY
1 : 950,000

	Motorway (under construction)
	Toll motorway
	4- or Multi-lane road (under construction)
	Trunk-road (under construction)
	Important main road (under construction)
	Main road
	Side road
	Railway
	Prohibited area
	National Park and nature reserve
4 2 A22	Motorway number
E54	E-Road number
34 28 N22 66	Other street numbers
22	Motorway junction number
○	Motorway junction
	Unsuitable for caravans
	Prohibited for caravans
	Motorway petrol station
	Motorway services
	Motorway services with motel
	Major airport
	Airport
	Airfield
	Car ferry

KEY

The maps on the following pages show Scotland on a scale of 1:950,000. Geographical details have been supplemented by numerous items of useful information: the traffic and transport system has been mapped out in great detail and symbols indicate all the important sights and tourist destinations by location and type. The names of cities that tourists may find particularly interesting are highlighted in yellow. UNESCO World Natural Heritage Sites are specially marked for convenience.

SYMBOLS

Auto route
Rail road
UNESCO World Heritage (Natural)
Mountain landscape
Rock landscape
Ravine/canyon
Cave
River landscape
Waterfall/rapids
Lake country
Nature park
National Park (landscape)
National Park (Flora)
National Park (fauna)
National Park (culture)
Whale watching
Zoo
Botanical garden
Coastal landscape
Island
Beach
UNESCO World Heritage (Cultural)
Remarkable city
Pre- and early history

Roman antiquity
Places of Christian cultural interest
Christian monastery
Cultural landscape
Historic cityscape
Castle/fortress/fort
Castle ruins
Palace
Technical/industrial monument
Lighthouse worth seeing
Remarkable bridge
Tomb/grave
Theatre of war/battlefield
Monument
Open-air museum
Information centre
Abandoned mine
Remarkable tower
Market/bazaar
Festivals
Museum
Theatre
World exhibition

Race track
Golf
Horse racing
Skiing
Sailing
Diving
Wind surfing
Surfing
Seaport
Beach resort
Mineral/thermal spa
Amusement/theme park
Casino
Hiking area
Viewing point
Mountain railway
Shipwreck

Additional symbols for the Index

Place/town
Capital
Province
Capital of the province

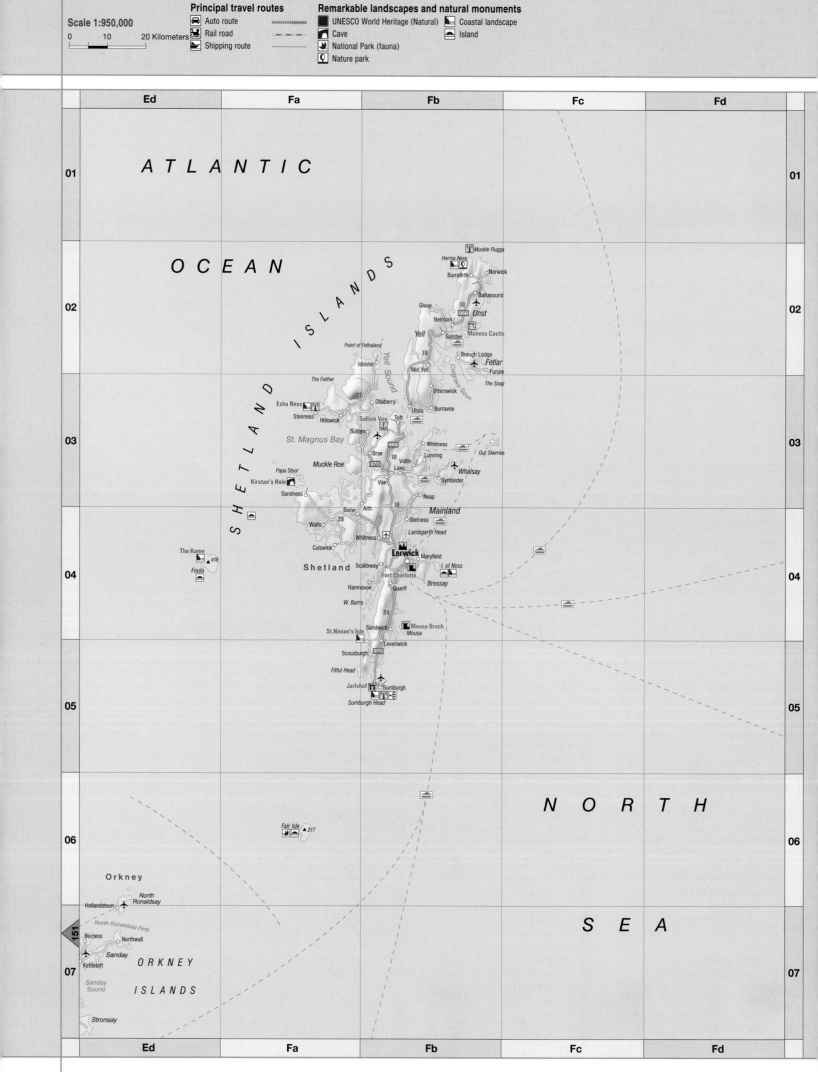

Principal travel routes

🚗 Auto route
🚂 Rail road   ⋯⋯⋯⋯⋯
🚢 Shipping route   ————

Remarkable landscapes and natural monuments

■ UNESCO World Heritage (Natural)   ▪ Coastal landscape
▪ Cave   ▪ Island
▪ National Park (fauna)
◉ Nature park

	Ed	Fa	Fb	Fc	Fd

ATLANTIC

OCEAN

SHETLAND ISLANDS

🏰 Muckle Flugga
Herma Ness 🏰
Burrafirth   • Norwick
              • Baltasound
Gloup   10
Belmont   968   *Unst*
        Gutcher   🏰 Muness Castle
Point of Fethaland
                18   Brough Lodge ✈
Isbister   *Fetlar*
Yell Sound   Mid Yell   • Funzie
The Faither   *The Snap*
                        Otterswick
Esha Ness 🏰   • Ollaberry   Ulsta   Burravoe
Stenness   Hillswick   Sullom Voe   Toft
St. Magnus Bay   Sullom ✈   Whitness
                     968   Lunning   *Out Skerries*
Papa Stour   Brae   10   Vidlin   🏰 Whalsay
Kirstan's Hole 🏰   970   Laxo   Symbister
Sandness   Voe   Neap
Muckle Roe
                 Bixter   Aith   18   Gletness
          Walls   29   *Mainland*
The Kame 🏰   Whitness ✈   Lambgarth Head
        ▲418   • Maryfield
Foula   Culswick   **Lerwick**   *I. of Noss*
        Scalloway   🏰   *Bressay*
Shetland   Fort Charlotte
        Hamnavoe   Quarff
W. Burra   24
             🏰 Mousa Broch
   St.Ninian's Isle   Sandwick   *Mousa*
        Levenwick
   Scousburgh   970
Fitful Head
   Jarlshof 🏛 ✈ Sumburgh
Sumburgh Head

NORTH

SEA

🏰 Fair Isle   ▲217

Orkney
          • North
Hollandstoun Ronaldsay
North Ronaldsay Firth
   Burness   • Northwall
   ✈ Sanday
   Kettletoft
Sanday
ORKNEY
*Sanday
Sound*   *ISLANDS*

Stronsay

	Ed	Fa	Fb	Fc	Fd

151

Remarkable cities and cultural monuments

☐ UNESCO World Heritage (Cultural)   ▥ Castle/fortress/fort   ⌂ Castle ruin
▲ Pre- and early history   ▦ Palace
▲ Places of Christian cultural interest ▦ Historical city scape
▲ Romanesque church   ▦ Remarkable lighthouse

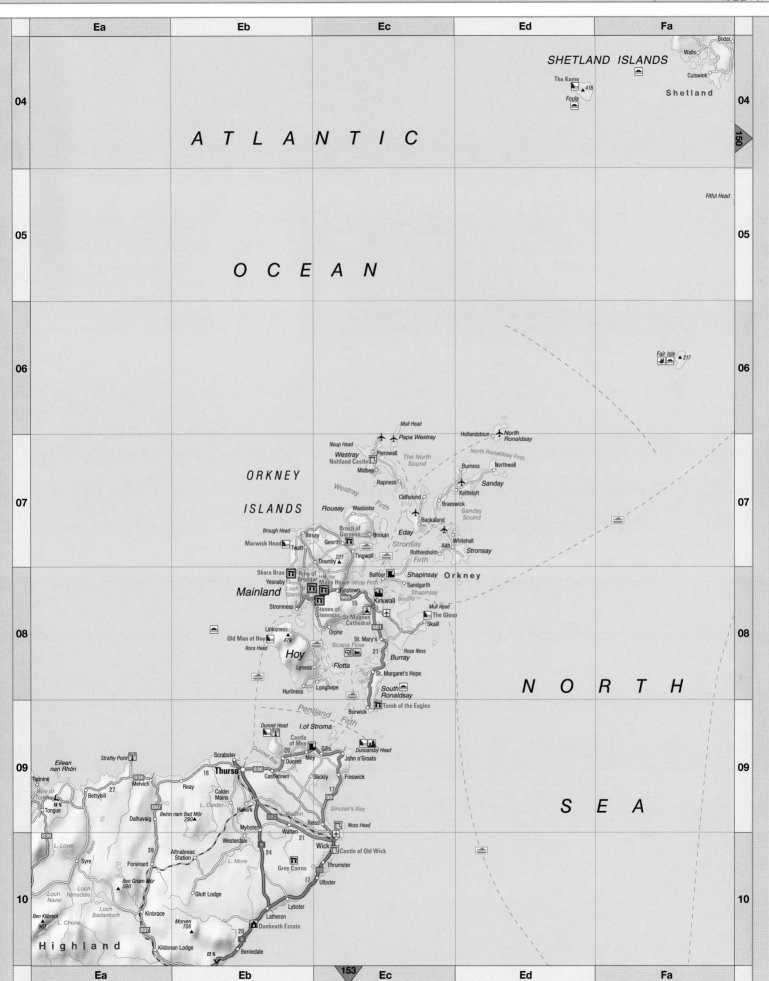

| | Ea | Eb | Ec | Ed | Fa |

04

A T L A N T I C

SHETLAND ISLANDS
Walls
Bixter
Culswick
The Kame ▲418
Foula ▲
Shetland
150

05

O C E A N

Fitful Head

06

Fair Isle ▲217

07

O R K N E Y

I S L A N D S

Mull Head
Noup Head   Papa Westray
Westray   Pierowall
Noltland Castle   The North Sound
Midbea   Hollandstoun   North Ronaldsay
Rapness   North Ronaldsay Firth
Westray Firth   Burness   Northwall
Rousay   Wasbister   Calfsound   Sanday
Brough Head   Birsay   Broch of   Kettletoft
Marwick Head Twatt   Gurness Brinian   Braeswick
             Georth   Eday   Sanday Sound
             Dounby ▲ Tingwall   Backaland   Whitehall
Skara Brae Ring of   Hray Stronsay Aith Stronsay
Yesnaby   Brodgar   Maes Howe Rothiesholm Firth
Mainland Loch of   Finstown Balfour Sandgarth
          Stenness   965 Shapinsay   Shapinsay
Stromness Stones of 15 Kirkwall   Sound
           Stenness St. Magnus   Mull Head
           961   Cathedral   Skaill The Gloup
Linksness Orphir
Old Man of Hoy ▲479 St. Mary's   O R K N E Y
Rora Head   Scapa Flow   21 Rose Ness
Hoy   Lyness   Flotta   Burray
         Longhope St. Margaret's Hope   N O R T H
Hurliness
                South Ronaldsay
             Burwick Tomb of the Eagles   S E A
             Pentland Firth
Dunnet Head I. of Stroma
Castle   of Mey   Duncansby Head
Strathy Point Scrabster 20 Mey Gills John o'Groats
Eilean   Thurso 836 Dunnet Slickly Freswick
nan Rhón   Melvich Castletown   17
Talmine   Reay   Sinclair's Bay
Kyle of Bettyhill Calder   Haikirk Watten Noss Head
Tongue   15%   Mains 897 882 Reiss 21
Tongue   Dalhavaig Beinn nam Bad Mór Mybster Wick
         ▲290   Westerdale 24 Castle of Old Wick
836 L. Loyal   Altnabreac Grey Cairns Thrumster
     L. Calder Station 99
Syre Forsinard L. More 17 Ulbster
Loch   Ben Griam Mór Lybster
Rimsdale   ▲590   Latheron
Loch Naver Kinbrace Glutt Lodge
Loch   Dunbeath Estate
Badanloch   897 Morven ▲706 20
Ben Klibreck Kildonan Lodge 9
▲961 L. Choire   13% Berriedale
H i g h l a n d

08

09

10

Scale 1:950,000

Principal travel routes
🚗 Auto route
🚂 Rail road
⛴ Shipping route

Remarkable landscapes and natural monuments
⬛ UNESCO World Heritage (Natural)
🏔 Mountain landscape
Ravine/canyon
Cave
River landscape
Waterfall/rapids
Lake country
National Park (fauna)
Nature park
Coastal landscape
Island
Beach
Zoo/safari park
Botanical garden
Whale watching

0   10   20 Kilometers

	Cc	Cd	Da	Db	Dc

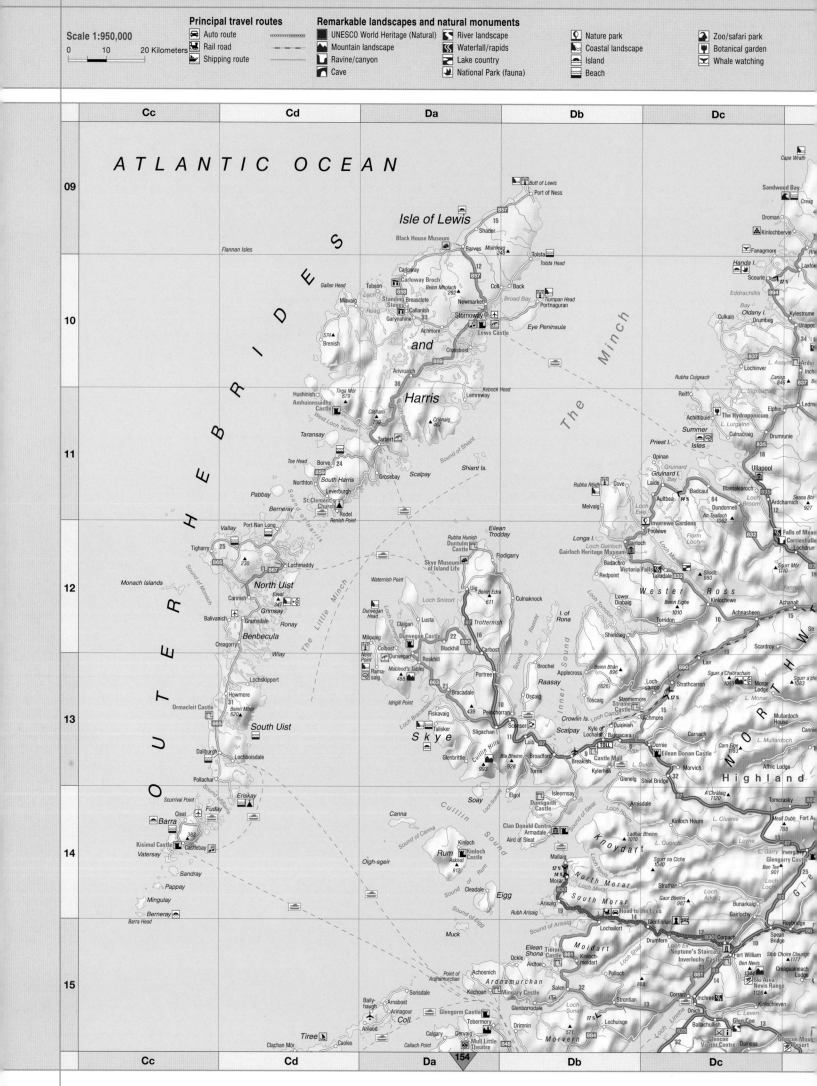

A T L A N T I C   O C E A N

Isle of Lewis

Butt of Lewis
Port of Ness
Shader
Black House Museum
Barvas
Muirhead 248
Tolsta
Tolsta Head
Carloway
Carloway Broch
Tobson
Beinn Mholach 292
Coll
Back
Miavaig
Standing Stones Breasclete
Callanish 33
Newmarket
Garynahine
Achmore
Stornoway
Lews Castle
Broad Bay
Tiumpan Head
Portnaguran
Eye Peninsula
574
Brenish
Crossbost
and
Arivruaich
859
Hushinish
Amhuinnsuidhe Castle
Tirga Mór 679
Harris
Lemreway
Kebock Head
Clisham 799
Crionaig 467
West Loch Tarbert
Taransay
Toe Head
Borve 24
Tarbert
Scalpay
Sound of Shiant
Shiant Is.
South Harris
Northton
Grosebay
Pabbay
Leverburgh
St Clement's Church
Berneray
Rodel
Renish Point

Cape Wrath
Sandwood Bay
Creag
Droman
Kinlochbervie
Fanagmore
Handa I.
Scourie
12%
Laxfor
Eddrachillis
Bay
Culkein
Oldany I.
Kylesrome
Drumbeg
Unapoo
L. Assynt
Lochinver
Ardvr
Rubha Coigeach
Canisp 846
Reiff
Achiltibuie
Elphin
The Hydroponicum
L. Lurgainn
Ledm
Summer Isles
Priest I.
Culnacraig
Drumrunie
Opinan
Gruinard
Bay
Ullapool
Rubha Réidh
Cove
Gruinard I.
Laide
Badcaul
Blamalearoch
14%
64
Dundonnell
Melvaig
An Teallach 1062
Seana Bhraigh 927
Inverewe Gardens
Poolewe
Fionn Loch
Falls of Meas
Corrieshalle
Lochdrum
Gairloch
Longa I.
Gairloch Heritage Museum
Badachro
Redpoint
Victoria Falls
Talladale
W e s t e r
Sgurr Mór 1110
Slioch 980
R o s s
Kinlochewe
Lower Diabaig
Beinn Eighe 1010
Torridon
Shieldaig
Achnasheen
Str
15
Brochel
Applecross
Beinn Bhan 896
(626)
Lair
Sgurr a'Chaorachain 1053
Sgurr a'chl 1083
Eilean Trodday
Duntulm Castle
Flodigarry
Skye Museum of Island Life
Uig
Beinn Edra 611
Culnaknock
I. of Rona
Monar Lodge
Waternish Point
Loch Snizort
Trotternish
Raasay
Stromeferry Castle
12%
L. Monar
Dunvegan Head
Lusta
16
Portree
Oscaig
Toscaig
Stromeferry
15
Mullardoch House
Claigan
22
Blackhill
Sound of Raasay
Lochcarron
Carnach
Cannle
Dunvegan Castle
Carbost
Applecross
Achmore
Carn Eige 1183
L. Mullardoch
Milovaig
Colbost
Roskhill
21
Crowlin Is.
Balmacara
Neist Point
Dunvegan
Bracadale
Loch Carron
Kyle of Lochalsh
Affric Lodge
H i g h l a n d
Ramasaig
Macleod's Tables 488
Fiskavaig
439
Peinchorran
10
Quirining
Dornie
Eilean Donan Castle
Morvich
32
Idrigill Point
Talisker
Sligachan
Scalpay
TOLL
Castle Moil
L. Duich
A'Chràlaig 1120
Tomcrasky
S k y e
Glenbrittle
Cuillin Hills
9
Bla Bheinn 928
Broadford
Breakish
Kylerhea
Shiel Bridge
Glenelg
Loch Long
Loch Cluanie
Meall Dubh 788
L. Garry Inverg
Glengarry Castle
993
Torrin
Isleornsay
Soay
Arnisdale
Kinloch Hourn
L. Quoich
Loyne
Elgol
Cuillin Sound
Dunsgaith Castle
Ladhar Bheinn 1010
Sgurr na Ciche 1040
Loch Arkaig
Bunarkaig
Gairlochy
Canna
Clan Donald Centre
Armadale
Aird of Sleat
K n o y d a r t
Ben Tee 901
25
Sound of Canna
Kinloch
Kinloch Castle
Askival 812
Gaor Bheinn 987
Roybridge
R u m
North Morar
Mallaig
Loch Nevis
Strathan
Spean Bridge
Oigh-sgeir
Cleadale
12%
14%
Morar
South Morar
Loch Morar
86
Eigg
Arisaig
Road to the Isles
Glenfinnan
Rubh Arisaig
19
Loch Eil
Corpach
Muck
Sound of Arisaig
Lochailort
Drumfern
Neptune's Staircase
Fort William
Inverlochy Castle
Eilean Shona
Tioram Castle
861
Kinlochmoidart
Loch Shiel
Stob Choire Claurigh 1177
Ockle
M o i d a r t
Polloch
Ben Nevis 1344
Creaguaineach Lodge
Achosnich
Achateny
Kilchoan
Minnary Castle
Salen
32
Ski Area Nevis Range 1128
Kinlochleven
Point of Ardnamurchan
A r d n a m u r c h a n
Strontian
13
Corran
Inchree
Onich
L. Leven
Glen Coe
Glencoe Visitor Centre
Glencoe Moun Resort
Baily-haugh
Arnabost
Arinagour
Glengorm Castle
Tobermory
Drimnin
571
Loch Sunart
17%
Glenborrodale
M o r v e r n
Ballachulish
Dalness
C o l l
Calgary
Dervaig
Mull Little Theatre
848
Lochuisge
Loch Linnhe
Tiree
Clachan Mór
Caoles
Caliach Point

Cc	Cd	Da	Db	Dc

154

Remarkable cities and cultural monuments

UNESCO World Heritage (Cultural)
Pre- and early history
Places of Christian cultural interest
Christian monastery

Castle/fortress/fort
Palace
Technical/industrial monument
Historical city scape

Festivals
Museum
Monument
Tomb/grave

Theater/theatre of war/battlefield
Remarkable lighthouse
Open-air museum
Castle ruin

Sport and leisure destinations

Golf
Skiing
Sailing
Wind surfing

151

Tomb of the Eagles
Burwick
Pentland Firth
Dunnet Head
I. of Stroma
Castle of Mey
Scrabster
Dunnet
Mey
Gills
Duncansby Head
John o'Groats
Thurso
Castletown
Slickly
Freswick
Melvich
Reay
Calder Mains
Halkirk
Slickly
Freswick
Strathy Point
Whiten Head
Eilean nan Rhón
Talmine
Bettyhill
L. Calder
Watten
Sinclair's Bay
Beinn nam Bad Mór 290
Mybster
Westerdale
Watten
Noss Head
Tongue
Kyle of Tongue
Dalhavaig
Altnabreac Station
Reiss
Wick
Castle of Old Wick
Syre
Forsinard
L. More
Grey Cairns
Thrumster
Ben Griam Mór 590
Glutt Lodge
Ulbster
Loch Naver
Ben Klibreck 961
Loch Rimsdale
Loch Badanloch
Kinbrace
Lybster
Crask Inn
Morven 706
Latheron
Dunbeath Estate
Kildonan Lodge
Berriedale
Colaboll
Lairg
Helmsdale
Lothmore
Helmsdale
Cassley
Ben Horn 521
Brora
Rogart
Shin Falls
Pittentrail
Dunrobin Castle
Golspie
Inveran
Achvaich
Littleferry
Skelbo Castle
Bonar Bridge
Evelix
Dornoch
Dornoch Castle
Fearn Lodge
Skibo Castle
Tarbat Ness
Tain
St Duthus's Chapel
Portmahomack
Easter Ross
Edderton
Hill of Fearn
Balintore
L. Glass
Milton
Alness
Invergordon
Balnapaling
Cromarty
Burghead
Lossiemouth
Duffus
Findhorn
Spey Bay
Portknockie
Findochty
Cullen
Kinloss
Cathedral
Elgin
Spey Bay
Buckie
Portsoy
Banff
Macduff
Gardenstown
Rosehearty
Kinnaird Head
Fraserburgh
Dingwall
Black Isle
Fortrose
Nairn
Brodie Castle
Alves
Sueno's Stone
Forres
Mosstodloch
Fochabers
Whisky Trail
Duff House
The Pole of Law
Cornhill
Loganmuir
New Aberdour
St. Combs
Fort George
Avoch
Clephanton
Brodie Castle
Dallas
Mulben
Keith
Aberchirder
Marnoch
Turriff
Cuminestown
New Pitsligo
Strichen
Rathen
Tore
Kessock
INVERNESS
Croy
Cawdor Castle
Ferness
Rothes
Craigellachie
Farmtown
Cuminestown
Old Deer
St. Fergus
Peterhead
Culloden Battlefield
Carn nan tri-tighearnan 1083
Moray
Archiestown
Aberlour
Glenfiddich Distillery
Cairnborrow
Huntly Castle
Aucharnie
New Deer
Buchan
Dores
Carn Kitty 521
Dufftown
Huntly
Badenscoth
Fyvie Castle
Methlick
Kinknockie
Boddam
Balnafoich
Marypark
Deveron
Kirkton of Culsalmond
Fyvie
Haddo House
Cruden Bay
Slains Castle
Tomatin
Ben Rinnes 840
Leith Hall
Insch
Tolquhon Castle
Ellon
Dava
Lochindorb
Rhynie
Cabrach
Oldmeldrum
Pitmedden
Newburgh
Grantown-on-Spey
Glenlivet
Pitcape
Inverurie
Whiterashes
Boat of Garten
Tomintoul
Aberdeenshire
Kinkell Church Kintore
Newmachar
Duthil
Kildrummy
Massatt
Kemnay
Carrbridge
Kildrummy Castle
Whitehouse
Castle Fraser
Dyce
Aviemore
Inverdruie
Geal Charn 821
Glenkindie
Alford
Pitfichie Castle
Sauchen
Balmedie
Monadhliath Mountains
Corgarff Castle
Craigievar Castle
Tillyfourie
Dunecht
Highland Wildlife Park
Loch an Eilein
Ski Area Cairngorm Mtns.
Colnabaichin
Queen's View
Echt
Kirk of St Nicholas
ABERDEEN
Provost Skene's House
Garrie Lodge
Kincraig Castle
Cairngorms
Morven 871
Tarland
Drum Castle
Girdle Ness
Kingussie
Ben Macdui 1309
Braemar
Torphins
Peterculter
Newtonmore
Aboyne
Crathes Castle
Laggan
Ruthven Barracks
Glenfeshie Lodge
Dinnet
Banchory
Netherley
Lochton
Carn Ban 942
Braemar
Balmoral Castle
Crathie
Ballater
Victorian Heritage Trail
Strachan
Kerloch 534
Muchalls
Gaick Lodge
Inverey
Braemar Gathering
National Park
Mulick
Stonehaven
Dunnottar Castle
Ben Alder 1148
Calvine
Devil's Elbow (665)
Auchronie
West Knock 691
Fasque House
Fordoun
Dalchalloch
Beinn Dearg 1008
Mayar 928
Clova
Laurencekirk
Inverbervie
Blair Castle
Beinn a' Ghló 1121
Auchavan
Runtaleave
Edzell
Arbuthnott House
Kinloch Rannoch
Killiecrankie
Stralloch
Angus
Tigerton
Marykirk
Johnshaven
Tressait
Pass of Killiecrankie
Glen Clova
Edzell Castle
St. Cyrus
Tummel Bridge
Pitlochry
Blacklunans
Dykehead
Tannadice
Brechin
Montrose
L. Tummel
Grandtully
Kirriemuir
Caledonian Railway

NORTH

SEA

09
10
11
12
13
14
15

155

Scotland 153

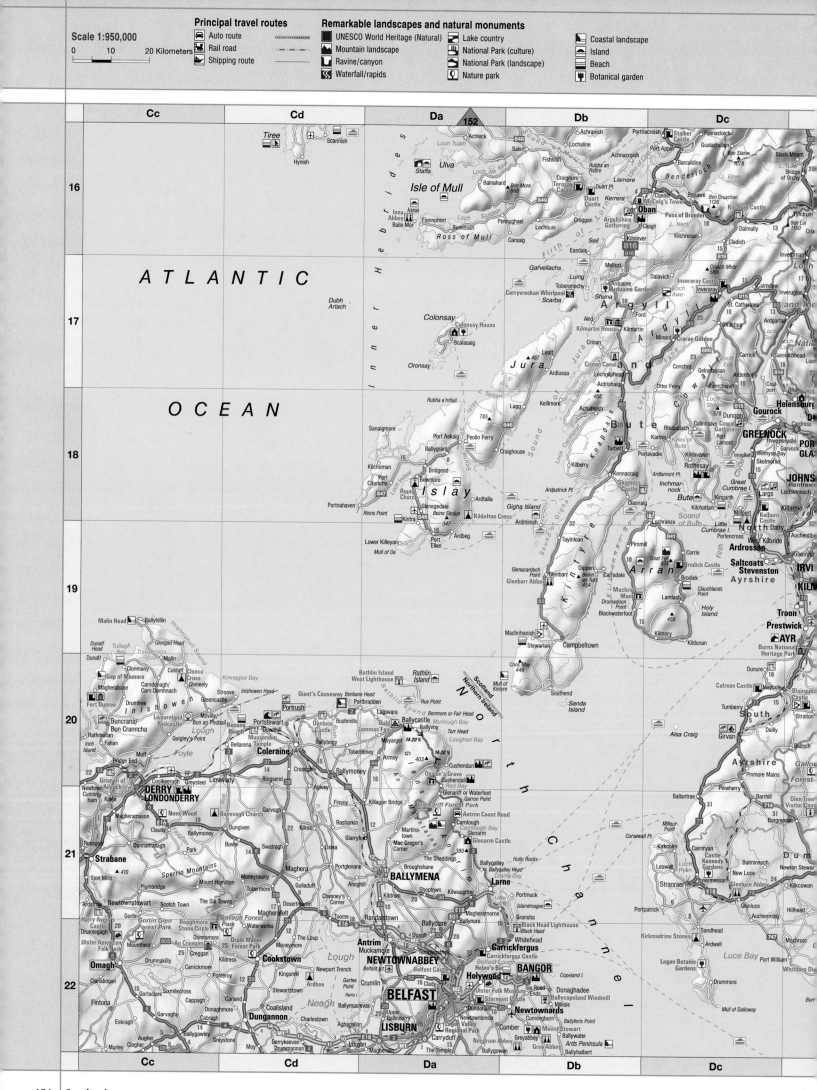

Remarkable cities and cultural monuments

- UNESCO World Heritage (Cultural)
- Pre- and early history
- Roman antiquity
- Places of Christian cultural interest
- Christian monastery
- Castle/fortress/fort
- Palace
- Technical/industrial monument
- Historical city scape
- Festivals
- Museum
- Monument
- Remarkable bridge
- Tourist information centre
- Castle ruin
- Worth seeing tower

Sport and leisure destinations

- Golf
- Sailing
- Wind surfing
- Surfing

Ea   Eb   153   Ec   Ed   Fa

NORTH

SEA

Castle Menzies
Taymouth Castle
Fearnan   Aberfeldy
Kenmore
Loch Tay
St. Fillans   Comrie
Ben Chonzie 929
Strathyre
Earthquake House   Dalchruin
Crieff
Drummond Castle Gardens
Muthill
Braco
of Leny   Doune
Callander
of Menteith
Dunblane
Wallace Mon.
Menstrie Castle
Ben Cleuch 721
Dollar
Clackmannan
STIRLING
Stirling Castle
Bannockburn
Alva
Alloa
Tillicoultry
Carron Bridge
Denny   Larbert
FALKIRK   Falkirk
Kilsyth   Slamannan
Kintilloch   **Cumbernauld**
Bathgate
North Lanarkshire
COAT BRIDGE   Blackburn
AIRDRIE   Harthill
Whitburn
MOTHERWELL
Newmains
HAMILTON
Larkhall   Carluke
Lanark
Strathaven
EAST KILBRIDE   Hazelbank

Dunkeld   Blairgowrie
Alyth
Rattray
Craigton
Glamis
Coupar Angus
Glamis Castle
Caputh
Little Glenshee   Stanley
Scone Palace   Forgandenny
Balbeggie
PERTH
Methven
Buchanty
Auchterarder
DUNDEE
Monifieth
Carnoustie
Buddon Ness
Tayport
Errol
Abernyte
Balmerino
Leuchars
Royal and Ancient Golf Club
St. Andrews
Newburgh   Newport
Elcho Castle
Dairsie
Cupar
Letham
Auchtermuchty
Ladybank
Myres Castle   Pitscottie
Kinross
Yetts o' Muckhart   Minathort
Crook of Devon
GLENROTHES
Leven   Largoward
Lochore   Kirkton of Largo   Crail
Kelty   Lochgelly
Cowdenbeath   **Methil**
Kinglassie   **Buckhaven**
KIRKCALDY
DUNFERMLINE
Culross Abbey
Kinghorn
Blackness Castle
Inverkeithing
Forth Rail Bridge
Burntisland

Kingsbarns
Fife Ness
Anstruther
Scottish Fisheries Museum
Earlsferry
Isle of May

16

17

Forfar
Friockheim
Inverkeilor
Arbirlot
Arbroath Abbey
Arbroath

Bell Rock

Firth   _of_   _Forth_

_N O R T H_

EDINBURGH
Musselburgh
Winchburgh
West Lothian
Ratho
Dalkeith
LIVINGSTON
Loanhead
Penicuik
Midlothian
Carlops
Leadburn
W. Linton
Blyth Bridge
Peebles
Neidpath Castle
Eddleston
Lyne
Castle Venlaw
Innerleithen
Walkerburn
Traquair House
Selkirk
Lauder
Stow
Heriot
Fountainhall
Oxton
Galashiels
Earlston   Stichill
Melrose
Newtown
Abbotsford House
Dryburgh
Melrose Abbey
St. Boswells
Waterloo Monument
Ashkirk
Hawick

18

Gullan   North Berwick
Aberlady   Dirleton   Tantallon Castle
Dunbar
Longniddry   Whitekirk
Ballencrieff Castle
Haddington   East Linton
Tranent   Spott
Pencaitland   Stenton
Gifford   Garvald
Humbie   Oldhamstocks
Longformacus
Westruther
Greenlaw
Gordon
Eccles
Kelso   Kilham
Floors Castle
Berwick-upon-Tweed

Barns Ness
Cockburnspath
St. Abb's Head
St. Abbs
Ayton
Chirnside
Duns   Coldstream
Cornhill-on-Tweed
Ford

Holy Island
Lindisfarne Priory and Castle
Farne Is.
Fenwick
Bamburgh
Bamburgh Castle
Seahouses

19

_S O U T H E R N   U P L A N D S_

New Cumnock
Kirkconnel
Sanquhar
Wanlockhead
Elvanfoot
Wiston
Abington
Crawfordjohn   Moffat
Colt Hill 598
Thornhill
Monaive
Kirkland
Knowehead   Closeburn
Parkgate
Lochmaben   Lockerbie
DUMFRIES
Torthorwald
Dalton   Kirtlebridge
Ruthwell
Sweetheart Abbey   Annan
Caerlaverock Castle   Gretna
New Abbey
Bowness-on-Solway

Traquair House
Tweedsmuir
Grey Mare's Tail
Loch Fell 688
Capplecleuch
St. Mary's Loch
Ettrickbridge
Tushielaw
Buccleuch
Roberton   Denholm
Bonchester Bridge
Stobs Castle
Eskdalemuir
Fiddleton
Saughtree
Old Castleton
Newcastleton
Langholm
Canonbie
Longtown
Smithfield

Jedburgh
Hownam
Oxham
Camptown
Upper Hindhope
Byrness
Rochester
Elsdon
Kielder
Kielder Resr.
Scotland England
Forest Park
Bellingham
Whygate
Bewcastle
Gilsland
Birdoswald Fort
Hadrian's Wall
Housesteads Fort
Chesters Fort
Low Row
Hexham

20

Langleeford
Wooler   Chatton
Morebattle
Town Yetholm
Hethpool
Wooperton
North Charlton
Chillingham
Ilderton
Powburn
Prendwick
Alnham
Alnwick
Alnwick Castle
Edlingham
Alwinton
Thropton
Warton   Cragside House and Castle
Craster
Dunstanburgh Castle
Loughoughton
Shilbottle
Lesbury
Warkworth
Amble
Broomhill
Acklington
Widdrington
Druridge Bay

21

NEWCASTLE UPON TYNE
TYNEMOUTH
SOUTH SHIELDS
GATESHEAD   **SUNDERLAND**
Whitley Bay
Boldon
Tyne and Wear
Washington
Stanley   Beamish Museum
Consett   Chester-le-Street
Durham
Stanhope   Crook
Wolsingham
Spennymoor   Ferryhill
Bishop Auckland
Shildon   Newton Aycliffe
HARTLEPOOL
Seaham
Murton
Hetton-le-Hole
Houghton-le-Spring
Peterlee
Blackhall
Wingate
Sedgefield
Billingham

Ashington
Newbiggin-by-the-Sea
Morpeth
Bedlington
Cramlington
BLYTH
Seaton Delaval
Seaton Delaval Hall
Bedale
Ponteland
Newburn
Prudhoe
Whickham

22

Solway _Firth_

Maryport
Workington
Cockermouth
Bassenthwaite
Keswick
Derwent Water
Castlerigg Stone Circle
Threlkeld
Skiddaw 931
Bothel
Aspatria
Wigton
Thursby
CARLISLE
Dalston
Brampton
Midgeholme
Alston
Nenthead
Allenheads
Edmondbyers
Stanhope
Langdon Beck
Mickle Fell 790
Middleton-in-Teesdale
Penrith
Pooley Bridge
Temple Sowerby
Langwathby
Melmerby
Garrigill
Cross Fell 893
St. John's Chapel
Cow Green Res.

Cumbria   _Durham_

The entries in the index refer to the main text and the maps. Each index entry is followed by a symbol (explained on p.149), which indicates the type of sight referred to. The symbol is followed by a page reference to the main text. Finally, there are details of websites that will provide up-to-date information on the places of interest and the various sights described in this book. Most of the places described in the main text will also be found in the map section, which provides a wealth of further information for visitors.

Left to right: The Standing Stones of Callanish; the "Old Man of Hoy" on the island of Hoy; Inverpolly Nature Reserve; Eileen Donan Castle. Below: Bishops Bay on Loch Leven – source of inspiration for Sir Walter Scott (1771–1832), author of *Ivanhoe*.

Left to right: Iona Abbey; Oban; Isle of Skye; Kilchurn Castle; the Standing Stones of Stenness; coast of Unst (Shetland Islands). Below: A rhododendron ("Rose Tree") in the gardens of Abbotsford House, home of Sir Walter Scott.

Photo Credits

Abbreviations:
C = Corbis
ES = Erich Spiegelhalter
EW = Ernst Wrba
HK = Hartmut Krinitz
JM = Jörg Modrow
KHR = Karl-Heinz Raach
KJ = Karl Johaentges
L = Laif
MSK = Martin Schulte-Kellinghaus
P = Premium

numbered from above left (l) to below right (br)

Title Look/Wothe; 2/3 KHR; 4/5 HK; 6/7 Hackenberg; 7.1 KJ, 7.2 L/HK, 7.3 MSK, 7.4 EW, 7.5 Scottish Viewpoint/Alamy, 7.6 L/HK, 7.7 HK, 7.8 Look/Wohner, 7.9 P; 8 L/HK; 8/9 KJ; 10 MSK; 10/11 L/Harscher; 11 L/HK; 12 al L/HK, 12 ar HK; 12/13 L/HK; 14 al L/JM, 14 ar HK; 14/15 EW; 16 HK; 16/17 L/HK; 17 bl L/HK, 17 br MSK; 18 al L/HK, 18 ar L/HK; 18/19 L/JM; 19 bl KHR, 19 bc HK, 19 br HK; 20 L/JM; 20/21 Look/KJ; 22 Look/KJ; 22/23 L/JM; 24 Look/KJ; 24/25 Look/Wothe; 26 C/Kaehler; 26/27 L/JM; 28 al MSK, 28 ac KHR, 28 ar EW, 28 c 1. L/HK, 28 c 2. HK, 28 c 3. L/JM, 28 c 4. KHR, 28 al EW, 28 br HK; 28/29 MSK; 29 a ifa /Pan-stock, 29 m P/ImageState, 29 b ifa/Pan-stock; 30 ifa/Panstock; 30/31 P/Nägele; 32 ol EW, 32 ar HK, 32cl HK, 32 cr HK; 32/33 HK; 34 al MSK, 34 ac MSK, 34 ar ES, 34 c MSK, 34 b HK; 35 a KHR, 35 b KHR; 36 bl KHR, 36 bc MSK, 36 r KHR; 36/37 MSK; 37 L/JM; 38 a P/ImageState, 38 al C/Papillo/Austin, 38 lc C/Benvie, 38 bl C/Benvie; 38/39 Look/Wohner; 40 al MSK, 40 ac ES, 40 ar ES; 40/41 MSK; 41 bl L/HK, 41 bc L/JM, 41 br L/JM; 42 bl EW, 42 bc EW, 42 ar KHR, 42 cl ES; 42/43 L/JM; 44 ac L/JM, 44 cl HK; 44/45 HK; 45 a HK, 45 b L/JM; 46 MSK; 46/47 L/HK; 48 ac KHR, 48 cl C/WildCountry; 48/49 HK; 50 HK; 50/51 a P/Mon Tresor/Woodfall, 50/51 b P/Im-ages Colour; 52 al Look/Wohner, 52 ar L/JM, 52 cl C/Ergenbright; 52/53 EW; 54 ac L/HK, 54 cl HK; 54/55 HK; 56 ES; 56/57 o P/ImageState, 56/57 b P; 58 al L/HK, 58 ac KHR, 58 ar Look/KJ; 58/59 Look/Wohner; 59 ES; 60 a P/ImageState, 60 l 1. Look/Pompe, 60 l 2. MSK, 60 l 3. MSK, 60 l 4. MSK, 60 l 5. MSK; 60/61 MSK; 62 al MSK, 62 ac L/HK, 62 ar L/HK; 62/63 a P/Images Colour, 62/63 b P/Images Colour; 64 a 1-4 ES; 64/65 HK; 65 Look/Pompe; 66 al HK, 66 ac MSK, 66 ar HK, 66 cl HK, 66 cc Look/Wohner, 66 cr KHR; 66/67 HK; 68 L/HK; 68/69 KHR; 70 al KHR, 70 ac HK, 70 ar ES, 70 b HK; 70/71 HK; 72 bl C/Antrobus, 72 ar C/Antrobus; 72/73 Look/Wohner; 74 al L/JM, 74 ac HK, 74 ar KHR, 74 l 1. L/KHR, 74 l 2. L/HK, 74 l 3. L/HK, 74 l 4. L/HK, 74 l 5. EW; 74/75 L/JM; 76 HK; 76/77 MSK; 78 a ES, 78 l 1. HK, 78 l 2. KHR, 78 l 3. L/HK, 78 l 4. HK, 78 l 5. L/HK; 78/79 HK; 80 al HK, 80 ar HK, 80 cl MSK; 80/81 HK; 82 al HK, 82 ar ES; 82/83 L/HK; 83 a L/HK, 83 b L/HK; 84 al L/HK, 84 ac L/HK, 84 ar L/KHR; 84/85 L/HK; 86 al MSK, 86 ac MSK, 86 ar L/HK, 86 cl EW, 86 cc EW, 86 cr HK; 86/87 HK; 88 al P/Panoramic Images/Vladpans, 88 ar P/Im-ageState, 88 b MSK; 88/89 Franz Marc Frei; 89 L/KHR; 90 bl MSK, 90 bc ES, 90 ar L/HK, 90 l 1. ES, 90 l 2. HK, 90 l 3. HK, 90 l 4. KHR, 90 l 5. HK; 90/91 KHR; 91 r 1. MSK, 91 r 2. MSK, 91 r 3. MSK, 91 r 4. HK, 91 r 5. HK; 92 al HK, 92 ac EW, 92 ar HK; 92/93 David Robertson/Alamy; 94 al C/Antrobus, 94 ar C, 94 c KHR, 94 b KHR; 95 a KHR, 95 b ES; 96 P/Panoramic Images/Stimpson; 96/97 EW; 98 a C/Rastelli, 98 c ES, 98 b ES; 99 a ES, 99 b C/Rastelli; 100 al HK, 100 am HK, 100 ar HK; 100/101 HK; 102 al L/HK, 102 ac L/HK, 102 ar L/HK, 102 c HK; 102/103 HK; 104 ifa/ TravelPix; 104/105 Scottish Viewpoint/Alamy; 106 al HK, 106 ar HK; 106/107 L/HK; 108 a P/StockImage/An-celot; 108/109 a P/ImageState, 108/109 b P/Images Colour; 110 a KHR, 110 bl KHR, 110 br KHR; 110/111 HK; 112 bl C/Wood, 112 br C/McDonald, 112 b C/Karnow; 112/113 C/Woolfitt; 114 L/JM; 114/115 L/HK; 116 bl EW, 116 bc L/JM, 116 ar EW, 116 cl KHR, 116 cr HK; 116/117 HK; 118 al L/HK, 118 ac L/JM, 118 ar HK; 118/119 L/JM; 120 al L/HK, 120 am HK, 120 ar HK; 120/121 HK; 122 al ES, 122 ar L/JM, 122 c Look/Pompe, 122 b Look/Pompe; 122/123 b HK, 122/123 b KHR; 123 c L/HK, 123 b Look/ Pompe; 124 HK; 124/125 KHR; 126 al HK, 126 ac L/HK, 126 ar HK, 126 b HK; 126/127 Look/Wohner; 128 ES; 128/129 HK; 130 al L/JM, 130 ac EW, 130 ar KHR, 130.1 Franz Marc Frei, 130.2 EW, 130.3 KHR, 130.4 L/HK, 130.5 HK, 130.6 EW, 130.7 HK; 131 la H&D Zielske, 131 lc HK, 131 lb MSK, 131 r H&D Zielske; 132 al HK, 132 am HK, 132 ar HK, 132 l 1. HK, 132 l 2. HK, 132 l 3. KHR, 132 l 4. HK; 132/133 L/HK; 133 r 1. HK, 133 r 2. HK, 133 r 3. HK, 133 r 4. HK; 134 L/HK; 134/135 Look/Wohner; 136 al L/HK, 136 ac L/HK, 136 ar L/HK, 136 cl L/JM, 136 cr KHR; 136/137 L/HK; 138 al L/HK, 138 ac L/HK, 138 ar L/HK, 138 c HK; 138/139 EW; 140 al HK, 140 ac EW, 140 ar HK, 140 b HK; 140/141 HK; 141 a HK, 141 b KHR; 142 al HK, 142 ac HK, 142 ar HK, 142 bl HK, 142 br L/HK; 142/143 L/JM; 144 HK; 144/145 EW; 145 bl HK, 145 br L/JM, 145 bl Look/KJ, 145 br MSK; 146 H&D Zielske; 146/147 P; 148/149 P.

This edition is published on behalf of APA Publications GmbH & Co. Verlag KG, Singapore Branch, Singapore by Verlag Wolfgang Kunth GmbH & Co KG, Munich, Germany

Distribution of this edition:

GeoCenter International Ltd
Meridian House, Churchill Way West
Basingstoke, Hampshire RG21 6YR
Great Britain
Tel.: (44) 1256 817 987
Fax: (44) 1256 817 988
sales@geocenter.co.uk
www.insightguides.com

ISBN 978-981-258-868-5

Original edition:
© 2007 Verlag Wolfgang Kunth GmbH & Co. KG, Munich
Königinstr. 11
80539 Munich
Ph: +49.89.45 80 20-0
Fax: +49.89.45 80 20-21
www.kunth-verlag.de

English edition:
Copyright © 2008 Verlag Wolfgang Kunth GmbH & Co. KG
© Cartography: GeoGraphic Publishers GmbH & Co. KG
Topographical Imaging MHM ® Copyright © Digital Wisdom, Inc.

Text: Kirsten Wolf, Robert Fischer (www.vrb-muenchen.de)
Translation: Dr. Joan Lawton Clough-Laub, JMS Books LLP

Printed in Slovakia

The information and facts presented in the book have been extensively researched and edited for accuracy. The publishers, authors, and editors, cannot, however, guarantee that all of the information in the book is entirely accurate or up to date at the time of publication. The publishers are grateful for any suggestions or corrections that would improve the content of this work.